ESSAYS IN THE HISTORY
OF MATERIALISM

ESSAYS IN THE HISTORY OF MATERIALISM

by

G. V. PLEKHANOV

translated by
RALPH FOX

New York · HOWARD FERTIG · 1967

First published in 1934
by John Lane The Bodley Head Ltd.

HOWARD FERTIG, INC. EDITION 1967
Published by arrangement with The Bodley Head Ltd.

Library of Congress Catalog Card Number: 67-13646

PRINTED IN THE UNITED STATES OF AMERICA
BY NOBLE OFFSET PRINTERS, INC.

PREFACE

IN the three essays which I am giving to the judgement of the German reader I make an attempt to interpret and explain the materialist conception of history of Karl Marx, which is one of the greatest achievements of theoretical thought in the 19th century.

I am perfectly aware that my contribution is a modest one. To show convincingly the full value and importance of this conception of history it would be necessary to write a detailed history of materialism. Since I have no possibility of writing this, I am compelled to limit myself to a comparison in separate monographs of French materialism in the 18th century with modern materialism.

I have chosen Holbach and Helvétius from the representatives of French materialism as being, in my opinion, in many respects very important thinkers who have so far not received the attention they merit. Helvétius has many times been refuted, often been slandered, but few have taken the trouble to understand him. In the explanation and criticism of his works I have had, if I may be allowed the expression, to work on virgin soil. My only guide has been a few fugitive remarks which I have found in the works of Hegel and Marx. Of course, it is not for me to judge how far I have made proper use of all that I have borrowed from these great teachers in the sphere of philosophy.

Holbach, less bold in his logical conclusions and less revolutionary in his thought than Helvétius, even in his lifetime was not so shocking as the author of the book " On the Spirit ". He was not so feared as the latter. Holbach therefore was more leniently judged and people have been juster to him. Nevertheless, he also has only been half understood.

Like every modern philosophical system, materialist philosophy must give an explanation of two kinds of phenomena, on the one hand of nature and on the other of the historical development of mankind. The materialist philosophers of the 18th century, or in any case those of them who adhered to Locke, had their philosophy of history in the same degree as they had their philosophy of nature. To be convinced of that it is sufficient just to glance through their works. The historians of philosophy ought therefore undoubtedly to have explained and subjected to criticism the historical views of the French materialists, in the same way as they explained and criticised their conceptions of nature. This task has not, however, been solved. For example, when the historians of philosophy speak of Holbach they generally only pay attention to his " System of Nature ", and in this work only examine what relates to natural philosophy and to morals. They ignore the historical views of Holbach which are scattered abundantly throughout the " System of

Nature " and in his other works. There is therefore nothing astonishing in the fact that the general public does not even suspect the existence of these views and gives itself an absolutely incomplete and false idea of Holbach. If we take into account that the ethics of the materialists are almost always interpreted in a distorted fashion, then it must be acknowledged that many corrections are called for in the history of 18th century French materialism. It is necessary to note that the attitude we have mentioned is encountered not merely in general courses on the history of philosophy but also in the special histories of materialism, which by the way are still very few, such as the German work of F. A. Lange, which is considered a classic, or in the book of the Frenchman Jules Soury.

As for Marx, it is sufficient to point out that neither the historians of philosophy in general, nor the historians of materialism in particular, even trouble themselves to mention his materialist conception of history.

When the twig is bent in one direction it has to be bent back to straighten it. In the present " Essays " I have had to act in just this way by first of all explaining the historical ideas of the thinkers examined.

From the point of view of the scientific school to which I have the honour to belong, " the ideal is nothing more than the material translated and refashioned in the human head." He who wants to expound the history of ideas from this point of view must endeavour to explain how and in what way the ideas of this or that epoch were given birth to by its social conditions, that is, in the last resort, by its economic relations. The giving of such an explanation is a vast and fruitful task, the solution of which absolutely transforms the history of ideology. In the present "Essays" I am trying to approach the solution of this task. But I have not been able to give it the necessary attention, and for a very simple reason. Before answering the question why the development of ideas has been completed in this or that manner, it is first necessary to explain to oneself how that development has proceeded. In its application to our subject this means that to explain why materialist philosophy developed as we see it in Holbach and Helvétius in the 18th and in Marx in the 19th century, is only possible after it has been clearly shown what this philosophy really was which has been so often misunderstood and even completely distorted. Before building the ground has to be cleared.

One more word. Perhaps the reader will find that I have not dwelt in sufficient detail on the theory of knowledge of the thinkers examined in the book. To this I can reply that I have tried to explain exactly their views on this point. Since I do not belong to the supporters of the scholasticism of the theory of knowledge so fashionable at present, I have had no desire to dwell in detail on this completely secondary question.

GENEVA,
  1st January 1896.

CONTENTS

ESSAYS IN THE HISTORY
OF MATERIALISM

HOLBACH

HOLBACH

WE are going to speak about one of the materialists. But what is materialism?

Let us turn to the greatest of modern materialists.

"The great foundation question of all, especially new, philosophies is connected with the relation between thinking and being," Frederick Engels says in his fine book 'Ludwig Feuerbach and the end of German classical philosophy'. But "it could first be understood, and its full significance could first be grasped, when mankind awoke from the long winter sleep of the Christian Middle Ages. The question of the relation of thought to existence, a question which had already played a great role in the Middle Ages, the question of which precedes which, the spirit nature, or nature the spirit, this question in spite of the Church assumed a more sharp form than the question, was the world created by God or does it exist from eternity? As this question was answered this way or that the philosophers were divided into two great camps. The one party which placed the origin of the spirit before that of nature and therefore in the last instance accepted creation, in one form or other—made the camp of idealism. The others, who recognise nature as the beginning belonged to the various schools of material- ism ".

So, in the words of Frederick Engels, to be a materialist means to see in nature the primary element. Holbach would willingly have accepted this definition. So, for example, from his point of view the psychic life of an animal merely represented a " natural " phenomenon, and, in his opinion, for the solution of psychological questions there is no need to go outside the sphere of the investigation of nature.[1] This opinion differs greatly from those dogmatic statements which are so often and without foundation attributed to the materialists. True, Holbach saw in nature only matter or " different matters "; he still recognised the four elements of the ancient philosophers—fire, air, earth and water. It should not be forgotten that he was writing in 1781.[2] In exactly the same way he recognised in nature only matter or matters, movement or various movements. Damiron and other critics tried to refute Holbach by palming their own concep- tion of matter onto him, and starting from that concep-

[1] " Le bon sens puisé dans la nature, suivi du testament du curé Meslier," A Paris l'an I de la République, I, p. 175.

[2] " Nature in the widest sense of the word is the great whole which is the result of the assembly of different matters, their various combinations and the different movements which we see in the universe ". (" Système de la Nature ou des lois du monde physique et du monde moral ", Londres 1781. I, p. 3.)

tion, they proved victoriously that matters are insufficient to explain the phenomena of nature. The victory was easily won, but of course materialism cannot be crushed by such arguments.[1] Critics of this kind do not understand, or seem not to understand, that it is possible to have a quite different conception of matter from the one recognised as correct by them. In the words of Holbach: " If we understand by nature a mass of dead, qualityless, completely passive bodies, then of course we shall be compelled to look for the principle of its movements outside of that nature. But if we understand by nature what in fact it really is, a whole whose different parts have different qualities, which henceforth act in accordance with these different qualities, being in constant action and reaction one upon the other, which possess weight, gravitate to a common centre, whilst others go away from it, and move to the circumference, which mutually attract and repel one another, are united and divided, and which by their continual clashes and drawing together again

---

[1] According to Damiron, for example, matter has no capacity for thought. Why? " Because matter does not think, is not conscious, does not act." (" Mémoires pour servir à l'histoire de la philosophie au XVIII siècle ", Paris 1858, p. 409.) Charming logic! By the way, both Voltaire and Rousseau fell into the same mistake in polemising with the materialists. For example, Voltaire declared that " all active matter points to a non-material essence acting upon it." For Rousseau matter is " dead ". He never " could understand what is a living molecule ".

5

produce and decompose all the bodies visible to us, then we are not compelled to have recourse to supernatural forces in order to explain to ourselves the formation of things and of visible phenomena ".[1]

Locke had already admitted that matter might possess the capacity of thought. For Holbach this admission appears the more likely " even if we accept the teleological hypothesis, that is admit that an all-powerful motive force moves matter ".[2] Holbach's conclusion is very simple and really very convincing. " Since man who is matter, and who has no other ideas save of matter, enjoys the power of thought, would it not be more natural to conclude that matter is capable of thinking or susceptible of the particular modification which we call thinking ".[3] On what does that modification depend? Holbach here puts forward two hypotheses which appear to him equally likely. It may be assumed that the sensitivity of matter " is the consequence of its disposition, of the union natural to an animal, so that dead, insensitive matter ceases to be dead and becomes capable of sensation when it is animated, that is to say when it is united and identified with any animal ". For do we not see that milk, bread, wine are transformed into the substance of a man, that is of sensitive being? These dead substances become, therefore, sensitive when united with sensitive

---

[1] " Système de la Nature ", I, p. 21.   1781.
[2] " Le bon sens ", I, p. 176.
[3] " Système de la Nature ", I, p. 81, note 26.

being. Another hypothesis is that advanced by Diderot in his remarkable " Conversation " between Dalembert and Diderot. " Some philosophers ", Diderot writes, " think that sensation is a general quality of matter. In this case it is useless to seek the source of this quality which is known to us by its actions. In accepting such a hypothesis it is necessary to follow the example of those who distinguish two kinds of movement in nature; the one known as a *living* force, the other as a *dead* force, and distinguish two kinds of sensation : one—active, or live, the other —passive, or dead; then the animation of a substance becomes merely the destruction of the obstacles which prevent it from becoming active and sensitive ".

However and whatever may be the hypothesis we accept in regard to sensation, in any case, according to Holbach, " an immaterial essence, similar to that which the human soul is considered to be, cannot be the subject of that soul ".[1]

Doubtless the reader will say that neither the one nor the other hypothesis is marked by sufficient clearness. We are aware of this, and Holbach was no less aware

---

[1] " Système de la Nature ", I, p. 90-91. Lamettrie also considers both hypotheses almost equally likely. Lange absolutely unjustly attributes a different view to him. To be convinced of this it is enough to read the sixth chapter of the " Traité de l'âme." Lamettrie even thinks that " all the philosophers of all time (of course, excluding the Cartesians) have recognised the capacity for sensation in matter." Cf. his " Œuvres ", Amsterdam 1764, I, p. 97-100.

than we are. " The quality of matter " which we call " sensation " is in fact a puzzle hard to solve. " But ", says Holbach, " the simplest movements of our body represent for everyone who begins to think about them, puzzles just as hard to solve ".[1]

In a conversation with Lessing, Jacobi declared: " I love Spinoza, but it is a poor salvation he offers us." Lessing answered: " Yes, maybe . . . But all the same . . . Do you know of any better one? "[2]

Materialists like Holbach might answer their opponents in just the same way: " Do you know anything better? " Yes, and where is this better to be sought? In Berkeley's subjective idealism? In Hegel's absolute idealism? In the agnosticism and neo-Kantianism of our days?

" Materialism ", declares Lange, " obstinately accepts the world of sensual appearance for the world of real things."[3] He writes this concerning the arguments brought by Holbach against Berkeley. Lange gives one to believe that Holbach was ignorant of many very simple things. Let Holbach answer for himself.

" We do not know the essence of any being, if by the word essence is meant what constitutes its proper nature. We know matter only by the perceptions, the sensations and the ideas that it gives, and it is according to that that our judgements on it are good or bad,

---

[1] " Le bon sens ", I, p. 177.
[2] " Jacobi's Werke ", IV, S. 54.
[3] " Gesch. d. Materialismus ", 2 Aufl. p. 378.

in accordance with the particular disposition of our organs."[1]

" We do not know either the essence or the real nature of matter, although we are in a condition to know some of its properties and qualities according to the way it acts upon us ".[2]

" Relatively to us matter in general is everything which in any way affects our senses, and the qualities which we attribute to different matters are founded on different impressions, or on the various changes which they produce in us ".[3]

Curious, is it not? Old Holbach is speaking here in the same spirit as the modern representatives of the " theory of knowledge ". How is it Lange was unable to recognise an ally in Holbach?

The fact is that Lange takes all modern philosophy from Kant, and, like Malebranche, sees all things in God. Lange was quite incapable of understanding that even before the appearance of the " Critique of Pure Reason " people could exist, and " materialists " at that, who were aware of truths which are really rather old but which appeared to Lange as the greatest discoveries of modern philosophy. He read Holbach with his mind made up.

But this is still not all. Between Holbach and Lange there is undoubtedly a vast difference. For

[1] " Système de la Nature ", II, p. 91-92.
[2] Ibid., p. 116.
[3] Ibid., p. 28.

Lange, for the Kantian, the " thing in itself " is absolutely unknowable. For Holbach, as a " materialist," our reason, that is our science, is quite capable of discovering at least some of the qualities of the " thing ". And the author of the " System of Nature " was not mistaken on this point.

Let us try to reason as follows. We are building a railway. In the language of the Kantians this means that we are calling forth the appearance of definite phenomena.

But what is a phenomenon? It is—the result of the influence upon us of the " thing in itself ". So, in building our railway we are compelling the " thing in itself " to act upon us in a way desirable for us. But what gives us the means of influencing the " thing in itself " in this direction? Knowledge of its qualities and nothing else but knowledge of these qualities.

And it is greatly to our advantage that we can become sufficiently closely acquainted with the " thing in itself ". Otherwise, we should not be able to exist on this earth and in all likelihood would have to renounce the pleasure of occupying ourselves with metaphysics.

The Kantians cling tenaciously to the unknowability of the " thing in itself ". In their opinion this unknowability gives the estimable Lampe and all good philistines an indisputable right to possess their more or less " poetic " or " ideal " god. Holbach thought otherwise.

" We are told incessantly ", he says, " that our senses only show the outer shell of things, that our limited minds are unable to conceive a god. It may be so. But these senses do not show us even the outer shell of the Divinity ". . . .[1] " Constituted as we are, that of which we have no idea does not exist for us."[2] It is of course undoubted that Holbach's materialism, like all French materialism in the 18th century and, indeed, all materialism before Marx, has its Achilles' heel. The main deficiency of this materialism is the lack of any idea of evolution. It is true that in people like Diderot we find from time to time guesses of genius which

---

[1] " Système de la Nature ", II, p. 109. Feuerbach said the same. In general his critique of religion has much in common with Holbach's. As for the conversion of the " thing in itself " into god, we must remark that the fathers of the church defined their god in exactly the same way as the Kantians do their " thing in itself ". So, according to Augustine, god cannot be brought under any of the categories : " Ut sic intelligamus Deum, si possumus, quantum possumus, sine qualitate bonum, sine quantitate magnum, sine indigentia creatorem, sine situ praesidentem, sine loco ubique totum, sine tempore semp itenum ". (" We must understand god, if we can and in so far as we can, as being good without quality, as being great without quantity, as being creator without necessity, as presiding without throne, as being everywhere without space, as being eternal without time ".

Cf. Fr. Ueberweg, " Grundriss der Geschichte der Philosophie ", Berlin 1881, II, S. 102-103. We refer the reader who wishes to study the " thing in itself " with all its contradictions to Hegel.

[2] " Système de la Nature ", II, p. 113.

would do honour to the greatest of the modern evolutionists. However, these guesses are without any connection with the essence of their teaching. The exceptions only confirm the rule. Whether it is a question of nature, of morality or of history, the "philosophers" of the 18th century always show the same lack of a really dialectical method, the same domination of a metaphysical outlook. It is interesting to see how Holbach labours at fashioning some kind of suitable hypothesis for the origin of our planet or of man. The tasks which have been solved by modern natural science, saturated with the spirit of evolutionism, were insoluble for the philosophers of the 18th century.[1]

The globe has not always been what it is. Then it was formed gradually, by means of a prolonged evolution? No. According to Holbach it might have happened in this way: " Perhaps this earth is a mass detached at some time or other from another celestial body; perhaps it is the result of those spots or crusts which the astronomers see on the surface of the sun and which have from there been able to spread themselves through our planetary system; perhaps this globe is an extinguished and deplaced comet which

---

[1] A strange affair. Diderot, for example, is delighted at the moral philosophy of Heraclitus. But he does not have a word to say concerning his dialectics, or, if you wish, merely a few unimportant words concerning his physics. (" Œuvres de Diderot ", Paris 1818, II, p. 625-626. Encyclopédie.)

once occupied a different place in the region of space ".[1]

Let us now hear Holbach's arguments on the origin of man. Primitive man perhaps differed from present-day man more " than the fourlegged beasts from the insect ". Man like everything else which exists upon our planet and upon other heavenly bodies is forever changing. Without any contradiction it may be assumed that species are continually changing.[2]

It seems as though we are dealing with a pure evolutionist. However, we should not forget that Holbach recognises such a change as being likely only if we admit " a change in the condition of our globe ", whilst he was speaking not of movement around the sun but of emergence from the region of our present solar system.

Whoever does not admit this must, according to Holbach, recognise man as " an accidental production of nature ". Holbach, moreover, is far from insisting upon the variation of species. In his words : " If one were to reject all the previous conjectures; if one were to pretend that nature acts through a certain sum of unchangeable and general laws; if one were to believe that man, the quadruped, fish, insects, plants, etc., have always existed and will forever remain as they are; if one were to insist that the stars would shine in the firmament for all eternity, we should not object."

[1] " Système de la Nature ", I, p. 70-71.
[2] Ibid., p. 73.

So, according to Holbach, the existence of " a definite number of unchangeable and general laws " excludes any development.

Holbach continues:

" If one were to say that it should be no more asked why man is what he is than it should be asked why nature is as we see it, or why the world exists, we should not object. Whatever the system adopted may be it will perhaps answer equally well the difficulties which embarrass us . . . It is not given to man to know everything; it is not given to him to know his origin; it is not given to him to penetrate the essence of things or to get back to first beginnings ". Is it not true that these words of a " materialist " might readily be quoted by certain modern " spiritualists "?

Holbach numbers the following among the " insoluble " tasks: " Did the animal exist before the egg or the egg before the animal? " A sound warning for those scientists who have too lightly laid down the limit of scientific knowledge.

The opinions expressed by Holbach on evolution may appear unlikely. But we should not forget the history of natural science. Many years after the first publication of Holbach's " System of Nature " the great scientist Cuvier was still passionately fighting against any idea of evolution.

Let us go back to Holbach's teaching on morality. In one of the comedies of the now forgotten author Palissot, who was however famous in the 18th century, a character (Valeria) is made to say: " Upon the globe in which we live there is only one single mainspring in the role of a world despot—personal interest ".

Another character (Cariondas) answers: " I have deceived Sidalisa with a certain regret but I see clearly that it is a permissible thing ".

In this way Palissot hoped to pillory the ideas of the " philosophers ". " It is a question of being happy, no matter how ". With this aphorism Valeria expresses the author's view upon the philosophers' morality. Palissot, it is true, was merely a " wretched scribbler ". However, of those authors who in one way or another have examined " the materialist ethic " of the 18th century and explained its history, have many judged differently? With very few exceptions all the authors of the 18th century recognise this ethic as something shocking,—a doctrine unworthy of an honest scientist or a self-respecting philosopher. Hettner, for example, recognises people like Lamettrie, Holbach and Helvétius as dangerous sophists who only preach sensual satisfaction and egoism.[1]

But such judgements break the rule of historical im-

[1] " The sophists of materialist ethic—Lamettrie and Helvétius " (Hettner, " Literaturgeschichte des XVIII Jahrhunderts ", Braunschweig 1881, II, p. 388). " The dangerous side of materialism is the gratification of indulgence, of food, and the stimulation of the lowest sentiments of man " (Fritz Schulze, " die Grundgedanken des Materialismus und die Kritik derselben ", Leipzig 1887, p. 50).

partiality. The philosophers of the 18th century did not preach anything like this.

" To do good, to procure the happiness of one's neighbour, to help him, is virtuous. Only that can be virtue which prompts the benefit, happiness and safety of society ".

" The first of the social virtues is humanity. It includes all the others in itself. Looked at from the widest point of view virtue is the sentiment which gives to all human beings the right to our heart. Founded upon developed sensibility, this feeling makes us capable of showing to people all the good of which we are capable. The consequences of humanity are love, charity, generosity, forbearance, gentleness towards one's neighbour ".

This is written by Holbach.[1]

Whence arose the accusation we have mentioned, which, although it is unfounded, is everywhere taken for true, and why is this so?

In the first place it is simply the effect of ignorance. Many people talk about " the French materialists of the 18th century " but they are not read. Can we be astonished after this that a prejudice, having once taken root so obstinately, remains in the history of literature and among the reading public? There are, by the way, two ample sources for this prejudice.

[1] " La politique naturelle ou discours sur les vrais principes du gouvernment ". " Par un ancien magistrat " (Holbach), 1773, p. 45-46.

The philosophy of the 18th century was only the ideological expression of the struggle begun by the revolutionary bourgeoisie against the priesthood, nobility and absolute monarchy.   It clearly follows that in this struggle with the outworn régime the bourgeoisie could not show mercy to the point of view adopted by the ruling classes.   " Other times, other relationships, and other philosophers ", as Diderot expresses it in the " Encyclopédie " in the article on Hobbes.   The philosophers of the good old times who tried to live in the world with the Catholic Church did not have anything against morality which was based upon a so-called revealed religion.   The philosophers of the new times were striving at all costs to emancipate morality from any kind of union with what they considered to be " superstition ".   " For human morality," Holbach says, " there is nothing so dangerous as an alliance with theological morality.   To connect a morality based upon reason and experience with a religion which is mystical, hostile to reason, and founded upon revelation and authority, merely means to weaken moral teaching and bring confusion into it ".[1]

---

[1] " Système social ou principes naturels de la morale et de la politique.   Avec un examen de l'influence du gouvernement sur les mœurs." Par l'auteur du " Système de la Nature ", Londres 1773, I, p. 36. Cf. the Preface to the " General Morality " of the same author : " We shall not speak here about religious morality which does not recognise the right of reason, because it sets itself the task of introducing it by supernatural means."

This separation of morality from religion did not of course please everybody. It was the first reason why the ethics of Holbach and his fellow thinkers were submitted to censure. Nor is this all. Religious morality called for submission, the mortification of the flesh and the annihilation of passion. In return for suffering in this world it promised reward in the next. The morality of the philosophers rehabilitated the flesh, restored the right of passion and proclaimed that society is responsible for suffering in this earthly life. As later with Heine, the philosophers of the 18th century wished " already here, on earth, to create the heavenly kingdom ". This was its revolutionary aspect but this also was its incorrectness in the eyes of the then supporters of the existing social order.

" The passions," says the author of the " System of Nature ", " are the real counterpoise of other passions. We shall therefore not endeavour to destroy them, but merely to direct them. . . . Reason, the fruit of experience, is merely the art of choosing those passions to which we should bow for the sake of our own good ".

As for the responsibility of society for the unhappiness of individuals, Holbach says, for example, the following:

" Let it not be said that no government can make all its subjects happy. Of course it cannot flatter itself it is able to satisfy the insatiable fantasies of certain idle citizens who have no idea how to assuage their boredom. But it can and it should concern itself with satisfying the real needs of the multitude. A society enjoys all the happiness accessible to it as soon as the greater number of its members are fed, clothed, housed, can, in a word, satisfy for themselves without excessive labour all the needs which nature has made necessary for them. . . . In consequence of human folly entire nations are compelled to toil, to sweat, to water the earth with tears, in order to support the luxury, the fantasies and the corruption of a small number of madmen, of a few useless beings for whom happiness has become impossible, because their wild imagination knows no limits."

In his " Literary Correspondence " Grimm tells how after the publication of Helvétius' book " On the Spirit " there was passed from hand to hand in Paris some verses expressing the horror of all " honest people " in the following words:

> Admirez tous cet auteur-là
> Qui de l'esprit intitula
> Un livre qui n'est que matière,
> Laire, lanlaire, etc.

The morality of Holbach and of the other " philosophers " was " matter " in the eyes of the crowd which did not understand it and also in the eyes of those wiselings who understood it excellently but preferred " secretly to drink wine while openly preaching water ". This is enough to explain how and why materialist morality still to this day frightens all the philistines of all " civilised " nations.

But among the opponents of Holbach's morality there were " philosophers " in their turn, and these not among the least. Voltaire and Rousseau condemned this morality. Do they belong to the tribe of philistines? Rousseau, of course, does not. But with regard to " the patriarch of Ferney " the reproach of a certain amount of philistinism is not quite without foundation. Let us examine the points in dispute a little closer.

On entering this world man, according to Holbach's teachings, brings with him only the capacity of sensation. From this capacity develop all the so-called mental capacities. From the impressions or sensations experienced by man from the influence of objects upon him, some bring him pleasure, others suffering. Some he approves, desires their continuation or renewal, others he does not approve or avoids as much as possible. In other words man loves some impressions and the objects forming them and hates other impressions and whatever provokes them. But man lives in society and is therefore surrounded by beings similar to himself and, like him, sensitive. All these beings seek pleasure and are afraid of suffering. All that brings pleasure they call good; all that brings suffering, —bad. They call virtue everything which brings them permanent benefit, vice whatever in the character of their neighbour brings them harm. The man who does good to his neighbour is a good man; he who does evil—a bad man. Hence it follows, firstly, that man " needs no aid from the gods " in order to distinguish virtue from vice; secondly, in order to be virtuous, people must experience satisfaction from virtuous acts. Virtue must be pleasant to them. If vice makes a man happy, then it follows that the man loves vice. A man is only evil when it is in his interests to be bad. Vicious and evil men are so often encountered on earth because no single government troubles to see that its subjects should find their advantage to lie in justice, honesty and well-doing. On the contrary, the most powerful interests invite people to injustice, evil and crime. " And so," says Holbach, " it is not nature which makes people evil, but our institutions force them to be so ".[1]

This is the formal side of Holbach's moral teaching, transmitted practically in his own words. It cannot be said that his thoughts were always clear and exact. The statement that " if vice makes a man happy, then the man must love vice ", is a simple tautology. If vice makes a man happy, then the man already loves vice. Such inexactitude from time to time leads Holbach into making unfortunate mistakes. For example, he once declares that " interest is the only motive of human actions ".

In another place he defines the word " interest " as

[1] Ibid., p. 306.

follows: " We call interest the object on which each man, in accordance with his temperament and the ideas which are characteristic of him, makes his well-being depend. From this it will be seen that interest is never anything but what each one of us looks upon as necessary to his happiness."[1]

The definition is so wordy that it is no longer possible to distinguish precisely in what way materialist morality differs from religious morality.[2] The supporter of the latter might say that his opponents have merely invented a new terminology, that they prefer to call those actions self-interested which were formerly termed disinterested. However that may be, it is easy to understand exactly what Holbach wished to say by the words: " If vice makes a man happy, then he must love vice." He makes society itself responsible for the vice of man.[3]

Voltaire thundered against Holbach as though the latter were advising man to be vicious if that were to his advantage. This recalls the abbé de Lignac who made a supporter of the new morality answer the question " Are we obliged to be devoted to the interests of our nation? " in the following way, " Yes, in so far

[1] Ibid., p. 268.

[2] It is not just wordy but is at the same time a tautology merely expressing that man only does what he desires to do, as Turgot has remarked in speaking of the morality of Helvétius.

[3] " In a corrupt society one must oneself become corrupt in order to become happy ". " Système de la Nature ", II, p. 237.

as it is to our advantage ". But Voltaire knew more about this question than de Lignac. He had studied Locke carefully and could not forget that " materialist morality " was merely continuing the work of the English philosopher. Voltaire himself in his " Treatise on Metaphysics " expressed much bolder things about morality than anything Holbach ever said. But the patriarch of Ferney had become frightened, he feared that the people, becoming transformed into atheists or even into utilitarian moralists, would get too great an opinion of itself. " Indeed," he wrote to Mdme. Necker (Sept. 26, 1770) " the century of Phèdre and of the Misanthrope was better than ours ". Without any doubt. They kept the people under much better then.

But the cream of the comedy is in the following. Voltaire puts up this argument against Holbach's morality: " Society cannot exist without the idea of justice and injustice. It (providence) has shown us the way to attain this ideal. . . . Consequently, the well-being of society for all people, from Peking to Iceland, is the unchanging rule of virtue ". What an important discovery for the edification of the atheist philosopher!

Rousseau argued differently. He was of the opinion that a utilitarian morality is incapable of explaining the most virtuous human actions. " What is the meaning of going to one's death for the sake of one's own interest? " he asked, and added that that philosophy is disgusting which is disconcerted by virtuous actions and which contrives to get out of the difficulty only by inventing base aims and motives for acts of virtue. Such a philosophy, according to Rousseau, is forced to " degrade Socrates and slander Regulus ". In order to estimate the strength of this objection it is necessary to cite the following consideration.

In their fight against " religious morality " Holbach and his school have tried in the first place to show that man does not need the help of God in order to understand what is virtue.

" Surely people do not need ", Holbach explained, " a supernatural revelation in order to understand that justice is essential for the preservation of society, that injustice only creates enemies ready to injure one another? Surely God is not necessary in order to show them that beings united in society need mutual love and the rendering of assistance to one another? Surely no help from on high is needed in order to discover that vengeance is evil, just as also is the breaking of the laws of a country which, if they are just, have as their aim the satisfaction of their citizens? Surely every man who cares for his own preservation knows that vice, debauchery and excess are dangerous for life? Surely, in short, experience has shown every thinking being that crime is an object of hatred for his fellows (i.e. the fellows of the criminal.—G.P.), that vice is harmful even for those who are possessed by it, that virtue

24

brings respect and love to those who profess it? In so far as people give themselves the trouble of even thinking a very little upon what they themselves are, upon what are their real interests, upon what are the tasks of society, they will at once understand what are their obligations with regard to one another. Reason alone is sufficient for us to recognise our duty in regard to our fellows ".[1]

If " reason is sufficient " to teach us what should be, then the meaning of philosophy is clear from this. Philosophy must show that virtue consists in the correct understanding of our own interests. It must show that the most famous heroes of humanity would have acted in the same way as in fact they did act, if we suppose each one of them had in mind only his own happiness. In this way a psychological analysis is developed which is really partially degrading for Socrates and slanderous for Regulus. Rousseau's objection is not without foundation. But the citizen of Geneva forgot that " slandered Socrates " himself too often fell into the mistake with which the " materialists " are reproached. " What sort of horse, or yoke of oxen, is so useful as a truly good friend? "—says Socrates in the " Memoirs " of Xenophon. The " materialists " have hardly expressed themselves more " cynically ".

[1] " Le christianisme dévoilé ou examen des principes et des effets de la réligion chrétienne ", Londres 1757, p. 126-128. This book is called the most terrible which has ever appeared on earth. In fact it appeared not in London, but in Nancy.

The Greek, French, German, Russian representatives (Chernyshevsky and his pupils) fell into the same error. They tried to prove what it is impossible to prove, but what was merely the fruit of a lesson drawn from the life of society. In the 18th century in general they liked to prove everything. The supporters of religious morality in this respect were no different from the materialists. Sometimes they " proved " in very curious ways. Here is a remarkable example. Helvétius relates that in Rouen in 1750, on the initiative of a certain Jesuit, a ballet was performed " having as its aim to prove that pleasure educates the young in true virtue. In the first act appeared virtuous citizens, in the second military personages, in the third spiritual personages. Truth was shown by means of dances ". Personified religion must have danced with pleasure, and in order to make the pleasure the more exciting, the Jesuits dressed it in dancing shorts. Helvétius is not particularly astonished at this rare method of " proof." He only accuses the Jesuits of inconsistency. " They recognise that pleasure is all-powerful; but if this is so, then why not recognise interest as all-powerful? Does not every interest depend upon the desire for pleasure? "

In a certain sense interest really serves as the basis of morality. The moral development of humanity follows step by step upon economic necessity and adjusts itself to the real needs of society. But the historical process of this adjustment is carried on behind the back of man, independently of the will and reason of the individual. Behaviour dictated by interest is represented as being enjoined by the " gods ", " by innate conscience ", " by reason ", " by nature ". In innumerable cases this is simply personal interest, though it is not always so. When it is a question of " virtuous " actions, then the injunction proceeds from the interest of the whole, that is to say from a social interest. The dialectic of historical movement transforms the selfish interests of a society or a class into the self-sacrifice and heroism of the individual. The secret of this transformation is comprised in the action of social environment. The French materialists of the 18th century knew this and knew how to estimate such influence. They unceasingly repeated that education does everything, that man is not born, but is made what he is.

But nevertheless they very often looked upon and represented this process of moral formation as being a number of arguments repeated in the head of every individual and changing under the immediate influence of circumstances connected with the personal interests of the character in question. From this point of view, as we have seen, the mission of the moralist is self-defined. It is essential to preserve the judgement of individuals from mistakes and to show them moral " truth ". But what does this mean, to show a moral truth? This means to show where lies personal interest properly understood and to praise this or that quality of the spirit which is responsible for this or that praiseworthy action. In this way arose that psychological analysis against which Rousseau objected. In this way also arose those endless encomiums on virtue which Grimm called " Capucinades " (or monkish preachings). These Capucinades are particularly characteristic of some materialists, and a false analysis of motives and actions of others of the French materialists in the 18th century. But the lack of dialectical method makes itself felt in the works of all the materialists and harms all of them to the same degree.

Rousseau in his controversy against materialist morality often appealed to conscience, to " divine instinct ", to " innate sentiment ", etc. It would be very easy for the materialists to explain even " innate sentiment " as the fruit of education and habit. However, they, on their side, preferred to explain it as a number of considerations having as their basis a properly understood personal interest. According to Holbach, " conscience " may be defined as " man's knowledge of the effects which his actions will produce on others ". " Remorse is fear instilled into us by the thought that our conduct may bring upon us the hatred or irritation of our fellows ".[1] Clearly Rousseau could hardly be satisfied by such a " definition ". But it is no less clear that the materialists could not assimilate his point of view. To admit even one single " innate feel-

[1] " Système social ", I, p. 56; cf. also " La morale universelle ", I, p. 4-5.

ing ", would have meant upsetting all their philosophy from top to bottom. Modern dialectical materialism does not stand upon such a shaky foundation. It gladly recognises the grain of truth to be found in both arguments and has not the slightest need to refute, for example, instincts and feelings which are the consequences of physiological heredity.

So, according to Holbach, all moral laws arise from reason. But on what is reason itself based in discovering these laws? On nature, Holbach answers without hesitation. " Man is a feeling, understanding, reasoning being ". This is enough for reason to make us happy with " universal morality ".

It is not difficult to guess the psychology of this appeal to " nature ". Moreover Holbach himself explained what it is about. " In order to impose obligations upon us, to enjoin laws upon us, undoubtedly a power is necessary which has the right to command us ".

However, the philosophers of the 18th century were at odds with all the traditional powers. In order to get out of this difficulty they had to appeal to nature. " Can this right of necessity be disputed? Can the capacity of nature, the superior power of which rules over all that exists, be attacked? " All this at that time appeared quite " natural ". But nevertheless it is necessary to emphasise that Holbach, like the majority of his contemporaries, had in mind only the " nature of man ", and this is something different from the nature with which we are forced to struggle for existence.

Montesquieu is convinced that " different laws " correspond to different climates. He explained this mutual relationship very insufficiently and the materialist philosophers discovered without difficulty the inadequacy of his arguments. " Can it be claimed," Holbach asked, " that the sun which once shone on the freedom-loving Greeks or Romans is to-day shedding different rays upon their degenerate descendants? "[1]

But the basis of Montesquieu's thought was not altogether false. At present it would hardly be disputed that geographical conditions have really played a part in the history of humanity. Those who engaged in controversy with him had in general no conception of what Hegel called " the geographical foundation of world history ". Human nature was for them the key by means of which they hoped to open all doors in the spheres of morality, politics and history. To-day it is sometimes difficult to accept even temporarily such

[1] " Politique naturelle ", II, p. 10; " Système social ", III, p. 6-8. Voltaire, for his part, untiringly disputed this opinion of Montesquieu which, by the way, is not new but taken from ancient writers. Justice demands that we should say that Holbach often argues about the influence of climate much more superficially than Montesquieu. " Definite climates," he says in his " Système de la Nature ", " produce people so organised and so varying, that they are sometimes quite beneficial, sometimes harmful for the human race ".

30

a point of view, even with the aim of understanding a way of thought so common for the writers of the 18th century.

" The development of art ", says Suard, " proceeds by the same ways which can be observed in the development of the human race ". Certain historians of literature have seized greedily upon this thought. They declare that the author is speaking here of the hidden causes of human development which, independently of the will of a personality, give it mind or enlightenment in this or that direction. They believe that Suard has got out of the vicious circle in which the thinkers of the 18th century were caught. But they are astonishingly mistaken in this. The causes upon which depend the development of " the arts ", depend only upon " the nature of man ". " In the period of his youth man possesses only feelings, imagination and memory. He desires only laughter, songs and dances. Later comes maturity to which belong the passions. The soul thirsts for movement and excitement. The mind develops and the reason grows stronger. Both these capacities demand, in their turn, exercise, and their activity is directed upon everything which interests the curiosity, taste, feelings and needs of man ".[1]

Thus argues Suard. In our time all scientific investigators recognise that the development of the

[1] " Du progrès des lettres et de la philosophie dans le dix-huitième siècle " in " Mélanges de litérature ".

individual from the cell to the mature form represents to a certain degree a repetition of the development of the species. The embryo passes through phases which are connected with the condition of the various ancestors of the given individual. Something of the sort is also true of mental development. The psychological development of every man is a kind of conspectus of the history of the development of his ancestors. It follows that adaptation to environment, particularly to a social environment, calls for important amendments to this law which, by the way, in biology also is not taken as being the complete, unalterable picture.[1] In any case the development of the embryo is to a certain degree the repetition of the development of the species; but what should we say about a scientific investigator if he, when studying the laws of embryology, saw in them a sufficient basis to explain the whole history of a species! But this is precisely the point of view of Suard and with him of all the philosophers of the 18th century who only confusedly sensed the real law of the development of humanity.

Grimm is here in complete agreement with Suard. " What nation ", he asks, " was not first a poet in order finally to become a philosopher? "[2] Helvétius

---

[1] As, for example, the development of the caterpillar is to a considerable extent the consequence of its adaptation from environment independently of the stages passed through by its butterfly ancestors.

[2] " Correspondance littéraire ", Août 1774.

alone understood things more deeply, but we are not at this point concerned with his views.

Man is a feeling, thinking and reasoning being. He is created so and remains so through all his errors. In this sense human nature is unchanging. Is it astonishing that the moral and political laws dictated by this " nature " in their turn appear general, unchanging and unbreakable? These laws had not yet been proclaimed and it must be recognised that " civil laws too often contradict the laws of nature ". But these corrupt civil laws depend either upon " moral corruption, or the errors of society, or upon tyranny which compels nature to submit to authority ".[1]

Let nature speak and you will know the truth once and for all. Errors are innumerable, truth alone is one. " No morality exists for monsters or madmen; general morality is only created for reasonable and properly organised beings; nature does not change in them. Good observation is enough in order to draw from here the unchanging rules which they should follow ".[2]

[1] " Politique naturelle ", I, p. 37-38.

[2] Condorcet declares in disputing the completely opposed views of Voltaire (cf. " Le Philosophe ignorant "; by the way, the patriarch of Ferney often changes his views), that the ideas of justice and right are necessarily formed equally in all " sentient beings ", who are at all capable of mastering ideas. Thus these ideas will be all of one kind. " Certainly, people themselves often change ", but every rightly thinking being arrives at the same ideas of morality as at the same theorems in geometry. Moral ideas comprise the necessary consequence of the physical truth that people are " feeling and thinking beings ".

How to explain now, why this same Holbach wrote the following lines: " Societies, like all natural bodies, undergo transformations, changes, revolutions; they are formed, grow and decay like all beings. The same laws are not suitable for them at all times. What is suitable at one period appears useless or harmful at another ".

The matter is very simple. From all these considerations Holbach draws only one conclusion. Old or outworn laws (he has in mind the France of those days) must be changed. The age of a law is rather an argument against it than in its favour. The example of our ancestors leaves nothing in favour of the law. Holbach could only prove this abstractly by appealing to reason. He nevertheless adapts himself to the prejudices of the reader of that period and assumes the appearance of standing apparently on historical ground. The same thing applies to the history of religion. " Philosophers " have busied themselves much with this question. But with what aim? With the aim of showing that Christianity is extraordinarily like other religions. In this way they hoped to strike a blow at Christianity. If he succeeded in making a breach the " philosopher " was satisfied with this and showed no further interest in the history of religion. It was a revolutionary period. All " truths " announced by the philosophers (and often contradicting one another), had in mind an immediately practical aim.

Let us remark here that " human nature " has often led the materialist philosophers much farther than they themselves expected. In Holbach's words, " The difference between the physical and the moral man has been too often abused ". Man is a purely physical being. The moral man in Holbach's opinion is this same physical being, only examined from a particular point of view, in accordance with the behaviour conditioned by his organisation. Therefore Holbach says, " all man's errors are physical errors."[1]

Medicine (or more exactly physiology) must therefore give the key to the human heart and even explain the historical movement of humanity. " In a nature in which everything is bound together, in which everything acts and reacts, in which everything moves and changes, composes and decomposes, is formed and destroyed, there is not one atom which does not play an important and necessary role; there is no invisible molecule which, when placed in suitable circumstances, does not bring about tremendous effects. . . . Too much bitterness in a fanatic's bile, the too inflamed blood in the heart of a conqueror, the bad digestion of a monarch's stomach, a caprice[2] passing through the mind of a woman, are sufficient causes for wars to be started, for millions of men to be sent to slaughter, for the walls of cities to be overthrown . . . for desolation and calamity to be created for many centuries

---

[1] " Système de la Nature ", I, p. 5.
[2] Does not a caprice also consist of molecules?

throughout the surface of our globe."[1]   The famous
aphorism about the grain which got into Cromwell's
bladder and changed the face of the world is well
known.   This aphorism is nothing more nor less than
Holbach's argument about the " atoms " and " molecules " being the causes of historical events.   The
difference is only that the author of the aphorism was
a religious man who believed that Providence had
directed the fatal grain to the necessary place with the
aim of causing the usurping Protector to perish.
Holbach would not hear of God, but he readily agreed
with the rest.

There is a " grain " of truth in such aphorisms.
But the fact is that this grain is part of a whole truth,
as the atom is related to the whole of the matter which
fills the universe.   The grain is so small that it does
not bring us one single step forward in the study of
social phenomena, and if there were nothing for
historical science to do but to wait for a genius—La
Place dreamt of this—capable of explaining all the past,
present and future secrets of history by means of molecular mechanics, then we might sleep a long, unbroken
sleep.   Such a wonderful genius will not come soon.

Let us listen to Holbach : " If we knew the elements
which serve as the basis of the temperament of one
man or many men who comprise a nation then we
might by means of an experiment also discover the laws
necessary for them and the institutions suitable for

[1] " Système de la Nature ", I, p. 214.

them."[1]   But what, it may be asked, happens in this case with " general morality " and " politics in conformity with law "?   Holbach has not a word to say about this, but he comments with great assiduity upon all the moral, political and social laws which are deduced as essential consequences from the " nature " of man.

In Holbach's time mother nature was ruled in both politics and morality by just those laws which were suitable to the French bourgeoisie.   And this was quite natural.   For at that time the third estate proclaimed that it was everything.

Between society and its members there exists, in Holbach's opinion, something like a silent contract which is renewed every minute and has as its aim the mutual guarantee of the rights of all citizens.   Of these rights the most sacred are freedom, property and security.   This is not all.   " Freedom, property, security are the only bonds which tie man to the earth on which he lives.   Where these advantages have disappeared then there is no longer a country (Patrie) ".[2]

---

[1] Ibid., p. 106. Jules Soury makes a naïve remark in this regard: " This thought of Baron Holbach has been partially realised. Moral statistics, by the way, are evidently more capable even than physiology of giving the greatest services to the physics of the nerves " (" Bréviare de l'histoire du matérialisme ", Paris 1881, p. 653).

[2] " Politique naturelle ", I, p. 13-14, 38, 125.   " The great and chief aim, therefore, of men uniting into commonwealths, and putting themselves under government, is the preservation

Property is the soul of this holy trinity. Security and freedom are necessary for society. " It is however impossible for man to exist or secure himself a happy existence unless he makes use of the advantages obtained for himself by his own cares and his own personality. Therefore the laws of nature give to every man the right which is called property." Society cannot deprive man of his property, " since it was created for his preservation ". It follows therefore, that property is the aim, and freedom and security are the means. Let us grant this and examine this sacred right a little more closely.

Whence comes it? Its basis is the necessary relationship arising between man and the product of his labour. In this way the field becomes as it were a part of the labourer who cultivates it. For his will, his strength, in a word, " the personal qualities belonging to him, the individual qualities which are part of his personality ", are put into this earth. " This field watered by the drops of his sweat becomes as it were identical with him; the fruits which he produces belong to him in the same way as his limbs and his abilities, because these fruits without his labour either would not have existed at all, or would not have existed in the same form as they now do ".[1]

of their property; to which in the state of Nature there are many things wanting." (Locke, " Of Civil Government ", chap. 9: " Of the ends of political society and government ".)

[1] " Politique naturelle ", I, p. 39.

38

In this way bourgeois property appears to Holbach in the form of the product of the labour of the property owner himself. This labour theory of property does not, however, prevent Holbach from valuing highly merchant and factory owners as " benefactors who give their occupation and their life to society as a whole at the same time as they enrich themselves ".[1]

Holbach, however, was evidently near to a more correct, even if not absolutely clear, conception of the origin of the wealth of the " manufacturers ". " The worker who lives by his work," in Holbach's words, " continually increases the property of the entrepreneur ". It follows then that this property is produced not only by (what innumerable crowds of workers set manufacture in motion!) " the individual qualities proper to manufacturers ". Undoubtedly not. But what is the harm in that! " Manufacturers " and merchants are all the same very useful persons and should not a grateful society reward such persons with riches and honours? The harm, according to Holbach, does not consist in the indisputed fact that the " artisan ", that is the worker, assists the increase of the property of the " manufacturer ". What is unfortunate is that thanks to " Gothic and barbarian prejudices, manufacturers and merchants are not respected as they deserve ". The peaceful trader is a despised being in the eyes of the warrior who does

[1] " Morale universelle ", II, p. 429.

39

not understand that this person whom he despises " clothes him, feeds him, maintains his army ".[1]

Holbach talks quite differently of feudal property. He calls property owners of this kind, " the rich and lordly ", " too often useless or harmful members of society " and untiringly pursues them with his attacks. It is they alone who " threaten to destroy the fruits of the labour of their fellows ". They threaten the freedom of their fellow citizens, personally insult them. " And thus the right of property is continually broken ".[2]

We know that society, according to Holbach, was created for the security of property. But the social contract has in view only bourgeois property and should only have this in view. So far as feudal property is concerned society has only one obligation, to smash it to pieces. Holbach stands for the abolition of all the privileges of the nobility, of labour services, corvées, manorial courts, etc. Of course he makes no exception in favour of guilds and similar " privileges " and still less does he insist upon maintaining " the wealth of the servants of the faith ". He says of the nobles : " If a monarch should think of taking away their harmful rights from them and they should insist upon the sacred rights of property, then the answer should be that property is a right of possession upon a foundation of justice; that anything inimicable to the national

[1] " Morale universelle ", II, p. 240.
[2] " Politique naturelle ", I, p. 42.

happiness can never be just; what is harmful to the property of the cultivator cannot be recognised as a right but is merely a usurpation, a breaking of a right. To uphold the right of the cultivator is more useful for a nation than to insist upon the right of a handful of feudal landowners who, not satisfied with idleness, in addition stand in the way of works which are very important both to themselves and to society ".[1]

The nobles " do nothing ", they fulfil no function useful for society. This is the opinion held by our philosopher and upon which he pronounces his verdict. Once upon a time the nobles were called upon to wage war at their own expense. Then, quite justly, they enjoyed certain privileges. But on what grounds can they claim privileges in a society in which the army is paid by the monarchs and the nobility no longer undergoes compulsory military service?[2]

The time has now come when the proletariat is weighing the rights of the capitalist on the same scales which were used more than a century ago by the representatives of the bourgeoisie for weighing the privileges of the nobility.

We should not think, however, that the antagonism between the bourgeoisie and the nobility appeared to Holbach as the expression of a struggle between landowning and various kinds of industrial property.

[1] " L'Ethocratie ou le gouvernement fondé sur la morale ", Amsterdam 1776, p. 50-51.
[2] Ibid., p. 52.

Nothing of the sort. Holbach has no respect for movable property. On the contrary, for him also true property is landownership. " The ownership of land forms the real citizen ", he says. The condition of agriculture is the characteristic sign of the economic condition of any country in general. " The poor man " is first of all a land worker. " To defend the poor " means to defend those settlers who are oppressed by " the great ". Holbach goes so far that he is ready along with the physiocrats to transfer all taxes, whether direct or indirect, on to the land, in exactly the same way as he relates everything good or bad which is connected with any nation to the land. " War has as its aim the defence of landownership; trade is necessary for the circulation of the goods produced by the earth; the importance of jurisprudence consists in guaranteeing for the property owners their rights in the land ".[1] The land is the source of all the wealth of a nation and it is precisely for this reason that it should be relieved as quickly as possible of the feudal yoke that still weighs upon it. A new argument in favour of the then revolutionary aims of the bourgeoisie. For a person like Holbach the idea of " equality " did not imply anything at all enticing. It rather appeared to him as a very harmful chimera. Peoples' organisms are not the same. People have always been unequal in the physical, moral and intellectual respects. " The man who is weak in body and soul will continually be

[1] " Politique naturelle ", I, p. 179.

compelled to recognise the superiority of the stronger, more gifted man. The more laborious will have had to cultivate a wider plot of land and make it more fruitful than he who has received from nature a weaker body. In this way inequality in property and influence have existed from the very beginning ".[1]

The Abbé Mably was able to object calmly against such arguments that they are in clear contradiction with the starting point of modern political philosophy, that is the absolute equality of rights of all people, both strong and weak.[2] The hour of equality had not yet struck. Mably himself was forced to recognise that no human force could undertake the experiment of establishing equality without exciting even greater disturbances than those which it was desired to avoid.[3] The objective logic of social evolution was on the side of the theoreticians of the bourgeoisie.

Holbach was just such a theoretician of the bourgeoisie, to the very marrow of his bones, even to the point of pedantry. He thunders against " the Pope

[1] Ibid., I, p. 20.

[2] " If my physical and moral qualities do not give me any rights over a person less endowed with the gifts of nature than I, if I can demand nothing from him which he might not demand from me, then explain to me, if you please, upon what basis I can make the pretension that our relations were based on inequality . . . I must show upon what legal grounds I could establish my superiority ". (" Doutes proposés aux philosophes économistes sur l'ordre naturel et essentiel des sociétés politiques ", à la Haye 1768, p. 21.)

[3] Ibid., p. 15.

and the Bishops who establish holidays and compel the
people to idleness ". He argues that the successes of
trade and industry are irreconcilable with religious
morality " since the founders of this morality have
cursed the rich and excluded them from the Kingdom
of Heaven ". He, in his turn, thunders against " the
multitudinous crowd of priests, monks and nuns, who
are only acquainted with one thing, lifting their lazy
hands to heaven and praying day and night." He
condemns the Catholic fasts on the following grounds:
" Only those powers who denounce the Church as
heretical get any advantage from these fasts; the
English make use of them in order to sell their cod
fish, while the Dutch get rid of their herring profit-
ably ".[1] All this, of course, is " natural ".

But when Holbach, like Voltaire and many others,
returns on every possible occasion to the story of the
two thousand swine possessed of the devil which were
drowned with the consent of Jesus, when he reproaches
the mythical founder of Christianity for his lack of
respect for private property, when he makes a similar
reproach against the Apostles who frequently plucked
the ears of corn from other peoples' fields, when he
for a moment reconciles himself with Christ because
" the son of man " did not observe the Sabbath, then
he becomes particularly pedantic and comical. The

[1] " Le christianisme dévoilé ou examen des principes et des
effets de la religion chrétienne ", 1767, p. 176, 179, 196, 198,
199, 203.

complete lack of historical understanding is seen in Holbach at every step.

The bourgeoisie, finding a representative and defender in the person of Holbach, appeared as the most just, privileged, noble, and educated section of the nation. The bourgeoisie of our day would have horrified him. "Miserliness (or, rather, greed for money) is an ignoble, selfish, anti-social passion and therefore not compatible with true patriotism, with love for the general good and even with true freedom. Everything is lost in a nation which is poisoned by this filthy decease ".[1] This is a tirade to the taste of Sallust, but at the same time we might be inclined to the statement that our philosopher had foreseen the scandals which are continually taking place in Germany (Struseberg), in France (Panama), in Italy and everywhere where the bourgeoisie has grown ripe for death.

" There is nothing in the world more terrible than a business man urged on by predatory greed once he becomes strong and confident of the approval of the country which encourages his useful crimes ".[2] Quite right. We know this better than our good philosopher.

Holbach most frequently looks at " riches " from a declamatory point of view. " Riches corrupt morals ". And now, having only just fought against religious morality in the name of wealth, he begins to fight against the greed for wealth in the name of " virtue ".

[1] " L'Ethocratie ", p. 124.
[2] " Politique naturelle ", II, p. 148.

" Only the most extreme vigilance," he says, " is able to prevent or, at least to hinder, the catastrophes which this passion brings with it ".[1] This is said by the very same philosopher who stands for the complete freedom of exchange. " Trade should be absolutely free, the freer it is the more it will expand ".

All that is left for a government to do for the merchant is to allow him " freedom of action ".[2] And now this very same Holbach argues that so far as possible politics should be directed towards preventing the multiplication of the needs of citizens. " Needs become insatiable unless brought within proper bounds ".[3] Here Holbach goes so far as to call for the interference of the state, becomes a protectionist, almost a reactionary. " We call trade useful if it brings the nations the elements necessary to feed them, for their most important needs, their conveniences and well-being. Trade is useless and harmful if it only brings citizens things for which they have no real need and which are only suitable for the satisfaction of the imaginary needs created by vanity ". Holbach would not hesitate before any measures in the struggle against this " vanity " which, according to him, even spreads into the villages by means of " lackeys ". In just the same way he was ready to fight against luxury as corrupting morals and bringing the most prosperous nations to

[1] Ibid., p. 145.
[2] Ibid., p. 150.
[3] Ibid., p. 151.

their doom.[1]   He considers the internal market, which ought to be guaranteed, as being the most natural market for industry.   Holbach is unable to understand the "senseless" mad drive to open new spheres of trade.   The consequence of this drive, he says, is that "the whole globe becomes too narrow for the infatuated merchant".   Nations often destroy one another for the sake of some barren island on which they imagine there is treasure.[2]   He cannot find sufficiently strong expressions to admonish "the people of Albion", who have thought out "the stupid plan of drawing the trade of the whole world to themselves and becoming the owners of all the seas".[3]   Holbach is afraid of too great inequality in the distribution of wealth, considering it to be the source of many evils. He supports the interests of the small farmers.   The English farms appear too large to him and here the farmer often becomes a "monopolist".[4]   In general, "the interest of the state is always connected with the interests of the majority and therefore demands that many citizens should be active, occupied in useful labour and enjoying a state of well-being which makes it possible for them to satisfy without difficulty the needs of the fatherland.   There is no fatherland for the propertyless".[5]

[1] "L'Ethocratie", Chap. VIII; "Système social," III, p. 73.
[2] "Politique naturelle", II, p. 154.
[3] Ibid., p. 155.
[4] "L'Ethocratie", p. 122.
[5] Ibid., p. 117.

47

It is easy to understand after this that the social condition of England, where the bourgeoisie had already carried through its " glorious revolution ", was far from pleasing our philosopher. He speaks of England with deep disgust. " It is not sufficient to be rich in order to be happy ", he says. " It is necessary to know how to make use of riches in such a way as to obtain happiness. It is not sufficient to be free in order to be happy; freedom should not be abused and unjustly applied ". In this respect the English leave much to be desired. " A nation without good morals ", " unjust to other nations ", " inspired with greed for gold ", " aggressive ", " inimicable to the freedom of others ", " a mercenary, vicious and corrupt nation "—such are the English in the opinion of Holbach, and he directs his teaching on virtue against them. " Britons, be wise and reasonable, strive to perfect your government and laws . . . fear luxury which is fatal for morality and freedom. Avoid religious and political fanaticism."[1]

However, the spectacle of the social life of England often inspired in him deeper considerations than those quoted above. He argues, for example, that the monstrous tax in favour of the poor has not lessened and could not lessen the number of poor in England. " It is too true," he exclaims, " that the nations among whom we find the greatest wealth contain a greater number of wretched than happy beings. It is too true

[1] " Système social ", II, Chap. VI.

48

that trade enriches only a few, leaving the rest in need ".[1]

All these arguments, to be just, are confused and contradictory. But let us insist on this once more, we are dealing with a theoretician of the bourgeoisie, inclined towards the spirit of revolutionary ideas and, we should add, inspired by noble sentiments. This bourgeoisie, or, more exactly, its best representatives, persons of mind and heart, dreamed of the rule of reason, of general happiness, of heaven upon earth. Was it possible for them not to be afraid of the fatal consequences of their own social tendencies? Was not this fear the inevitable source of their contradiction with themselves? Show to a young and beautiful girl an ugly old woman, bent with sickness. She will be horrified, but all the same the girl will be eager to live, that is to grow old, to become a fright in the eyes of others. An old but ever fresh story.

Whoever wishes to get a more striking idea of the French philosophers of the 18th century may compare them with great advantage to the Russian liberal writers, beginning at the close of the epoch of Nicholas I. The same lack of a historical sense, the same teachings, the same contradictions. Certainly, among these writers there were socialists, like Chernyshevsky, but there were others who fought against the " bourgeoisie " out of pure misunderstanding, merely because they did not properly understand the significance of

[1] " L'Ethocratie ", p. 146-147.

their own demands.   Many of our writers who considered themselves advanced went no further than
Holbach and his friends.   But they naïvely considered
this to be socialism.   The great Frenchmen would
have sworn that it was—philosophy.   As for ourselves,
we think that a rose would smell as sweet by any other
name.

In economic questions Holbach frequently agrees
with the physiocrats of whom he always speaks flatter-
ingly.[1]   However he did not share their passion for
" legal despotism ".   Holbach was a warm supporter
of representative government.   He did not recognise
French despotism of that period as being in any way
" a form of government ", but only an " unequal
struggle between a few armed persons and defenceless
society ".   Our philosopher asked himself some
" natural questions " which would have met with
sympathy in the Constituent Assembly of later days.
These questions are very characteristic.

" Should the whole give way to the part?   Should
the will of single persons rule the will of all?   Do
there exist privileged persons in society who are not
obliged to be of use to it?   Is the ruler free from the
ties of the laws which are binding on all governments?
Is the possession of force something which will never
be destroyed by justice, reason or another force? "

[1] " Zealous and virtuous writers ", " good citizens ", " it is
impossible to add anything to the views which inspired them
with love for society ".   (" L'Ethocratie ", p. 144-145.)

This recalls the famous words: " We, in our turn, will become conquerors ".

The following phrase recalls another scene from the history of the French Revolution: " The supreme power is nothing but a war of a single person against society once the monarch oversteps the limits which are prescribed for him by the will of the people ".

Uncompromising hatred for despotism inspires almost all the works of Holbach. It can be clearly shown that behind everything which he puts forward is not mere abstract theory but a painful reality. This reality, and not theory, forced him to invoke freedom, " the daughter of justice and the laws ", " the object of the love of all noble hearts ". You can frequently sense in him a foreboding of the coming political storm. " The citizen ", he says, " cannot, without renouncing his duty, refuse to take the side of the oppressed against tyranny ". Who knows? Perhaps these words before they were written were spoken in those philosophical meetings at Holbach's house where, according to Morelly, things were said which should have caused the thunder to break from above hundreds of times. Diderot, certainly, was sympathetic and even went further; Grimm, certainly, applauded . . . although he changed his views when, in place of the salon, the storm broke over the great historical scene.

How would Holbach himself have acted after the events of August? Finding himself in a Jacobin meeting, would he repeat his words: " The tyrant is the most hated being which crime can create "? To speak frankly, it is hard to judge. But it is more than likely that he would not have wished to have anything to do with these " wild " Republicans and would have considered them as being in their turn tyrants, enemies of the fatherland, fanatics and political charlatans.

Holbach respected freedom. But he was afraid of " noise " and was convinced that " in politics and in medicine heroic means are always the most dangerous ". He would willingly have negotiated with the " virtuous monarch ". Although, in his opinion, such rulers were rare, he nevertheless dreamed of seeing a sage upon the throne and there was a moment, during the ministry of Turgot, when he thought that his dream was realised. Holbach dedicated his " L'Ethocratie " to Louis XVI—" a just, humane, virtuous monarch, the friend of truth and simplicity, the enemy of flattery, vice, vanity, and tyranny, the restorer of order and morality, the father of the people ". It is possible that his opinion changed somewhat later, but the fear of " noisy " popular movements remained. The people for Holbach were the " poor "; but " need, frequently the plaything of passion and caprice, makes the heart fail or maddens it ". If the poor man submits quietly to his condition, " the effort of his soul breaks down; he despises himself because he sees on all sides scorn and derision ".[1]

[1] " The people which is compelled to labour for its support is not usually capable of thought ".

But it is even worse if he revolts. " It is only necessary to give a passing glance at the history of ancient and modern democracy to see that the people is usually dominated by frenzy and raging anger ". Wherever the people possesses power " it brings the principle of degeneration into the state ".

If Holbach had had his choice between absolutism and democracy he would certainly have declared for absolutism. Montesquieu, in his opinion, was greatly mistaken when he recognised virtue as the motive force of the republican form of government. The Republic bowed down before another idol, equality—" that romantic equality which in reality only represents envy ". Of all tyrannies the democratic one is " the harshest and most unreasonable ". In the class struggle which took place, for example, in ancient Athens, Holbach only sees " the folly of the crowd ". The first English revolution chiefly inspires him with horror because of " the religious fanaticism " of the people. The people is not created in order to lead; of this it is incapable. Freedom which goes too far quickly degenerates into license. The people is created for " practical labour ". Too great idleness " divorces it from work and leads it to profligacy ".[1] The people must be kept in " curb " and saved from its own " stupidity ".

[1] " Politique naturelle ", I, p. 185; " Système social ", III, p. 85.

A constitutional monarchy which grants freedom of action to the educated and virtuous bourgeoisie,—this is the political ideal of our philosopher. The bourgeois king (an expression often used by Holbach) elected by his fellow citizens and acting as the organ and executor of the will " of all ", while the propertied class is the interpreter of these manifestations of the general will, is what " nature " itself demands according to Holbach. Lange, the historian of materialism, is greatly mistaken in attributing to Holbach " a radical " " political teaching ".[1]

Radicalism was a psychological impossibility for the philosophers of the 18th century. We already know what is their idea of the people. They could have no other, since the French people, like the " matter " of the French metaphysicians, was a dead and inert mass. There remained, in consequence, only the philosophising and liberal minded bourgeoisie. Consistent radicalism which went to logical conclusions was a teaching far from suitable for the bourgeoisie as a class. This is just even for the most revolutionary epochs in its history (the French Revolution has shown this very well). But " thinking people " were only a handful of persons. Was it possible to recognise them as being a political force capable of shaking the whole social

[1] Lange, " History of Materialism ". By the way Lange only mentions " The System of Nature ". Evidently he had read neither the " Politique naturelle ", nor " L'Ethocratie ", nor the " Système social ", nor the " Morale universelle ".

structure from top to bottom? The philosophers saw perfectly well that there was no such possibility to be foreseen, and they therefore continually turned again to their vision of the sage upon the throne who should be capable of fulfilling their desire. Here is a remarkable and characteristic fact. When Turgot became Minister, the " radical " (as Lange considers him) Holbach, the uncompromising enemy of the despots, wrote that absolutism is very beneficial when it is a matter of getting rid of abuses, of destroying injustice, of correcting vice. Holbach is of the opinion that " despotism would be the best form of government if only it were possible to feel confident that there would always come forward in the role of despot a Titus, a Trajan, or an Antony ".

He could not forget that " absolute power often falls into hands incapable of applying it wisely ", but at the time it appeared to him that a new Titus had come to the throne of France. And Holbach asks for nothing better.

In order to reform society it is necessary to have a starting point. Where one does not exist even the " radicalism " of people discontented with the existing government is far from being uncompromising. We see this in Russia after the accession of Alexander II. When he attacked serfdom our " radicals ", like Herzen and Bakunin, declared themselves " vanquished " by the wisdom of the Tsar and drank the health of the Russian Titus. Even Chernyshevsky was inclined to recognise despotism as the best form of government if it gets rid of abuses, destroys injustice, etc.

The most brilliant and bold representative of the " Westerners " in Russian literature during the epoch of Nicholas I, Bielinsky, said a year or a year and a half before his death, that is at the most radical period of his life, that in Russia every progress comes from the top. Nicholas I resembled anyone in the world rather than a Titus or a Trajan. But what was Bielinsky to think? On what could he found his hope? From the West European point of view the Russian people was inert and dead matter which without a demiurge is nothing at all. When a few dozen years later a revolutionary movement began among our student youth, our " intelligentsia ", then a way out of the contradictions was found in the break with the " West ". The Russian people was declared to be riper for revolution and " socialism " than any other people. In this way the followers of Bielinsky and Chernyshevsky actually became Slavophils because of revolution.

" Many monarchs," Holbach writes, " rule tyrannically only because they do not know the truth. They hate the truth because they do not know its invaluable advantages ". The wise monarch " never begins jealously to preserve his unlimited power; he sacrifices a part of it in order the better to make use of the rest ". A few years back Madame Tsebrikova in her famous letter to Alexander III repeated this. Madame Tsebrikova was not in any way a radical.[1]

At the beginning of 1890 the German Emperor published his Decrees on the Labour Question. The " liberal " and " radical " Russian press were convinced that Germany was being ruled by " a sage on the throne ".

" The sage on the throne "—this was the deus ex machina of French philosophy in the 18th century. At one blow he solved all theoretical difficulties, all the contradictions engendered by the metaphysical point of view with which the " philosophers " examined all social phenomena. What was history for the enlightened Frenchman? An endless succession of for the most part very unfortunate events, without any connection, without any determining laws.

" From time to time you meet in history fortunate periods when knowledge, laws and good morals brought happiness to states. But more often you meet unfortunate periods when ignorance, prejudices, error and vice brought unhappiness to nations and destroyed the most prosperous Kingdoms ". Condillac, one of the philosophers, wrote this to his pupil, the Prince of Parma.[2]

---

[1] Tsebrikova asked the Emperor what history would say of him if he went on ruling as before. " What is that to do with you? " the Tsar wrote on the margin of her letter.

[2] " Cours de études pour l'instruction du prince de Parme ", Genève 1779, IV, p. 1-2.

Whence come such dark periods? They come from lack of enlightenment. " Arts and sciences born in the depths of barbarism gradually enlighten a small number of privileged nations. This is the light which is concealed from some in proportion as it is revealed to others and always illumines only a very limited horizon ".[1]

Voltaire in his " Essai sur les mœurs " expressed the same thought more shortly and strongly. " Reason ", he says, " is only found at the moment of arising ". Formerly there was much unreason, stupidity, and unreason and stupidity obey no laws, and in general " are not worth studying ". It is sufficient to state their existence. Speaking of the Asiatic barbarians, Voltaire remarked: " Their ancestors do not deserve historical description any more than the wolves and tigers of their country ".[2] But among the " philosophers " Voltaire was one of the best connoisseurs of history. He energetically disputed the view of his " divine Emily ", who was not in a condition to read any detailed work on the history of modern nations.[3] The great majority knew history much worse than Voltaire.

" Man begins," in the words of Holbach, " by eating acorns and fighting for his food with wild beasts and finishes by measuring the heavens. At first he

[1] Ibid., p. 2.
[2] " Essai sur les mœurs ", Chap. 53.
[3] Preface to " Essai sur les mœurs ".

simply works and sews, then he invents the measurement of the earth, that is geometry. To defend himself against cold he first covers himself with the skin of the beasts he has vanquished and after a thousand years is clothed in silk and gold. The cave, the tent —such were the first dwellings, but man finally builds palaces ".[1]

To-day, without mentioning Marx and Engels, we can quote Morgan who took as the starting point of development the productive forces of humanity and in this way successfully penetrated the secret of historical movement. Holbach did not even sense that he was emphasising the chief facts in human history. He enumerated them only in order to show the triumph of " reason " and because he wished to prove the error of Rousseau's view that the condition of a savage is better than the condition of civilised man.

" It is only through error that humanity has made itself unhappy ", in this is the whole philosophy of history of Holbach.[2] If he were compelled to explain in more detail he would say that ancient civilisation perished through " luxury ", and that the source of feudalism was " plunder, disorder and war ". He would say that the English revolution which cost Charles I his head proceeded from " religious differences, lack of toleration ", that " Jesus was a fraud ",

---

[1] " Système social ", I, p. 119.
[2] " Système de la Nature," I, p. 3. Cf. also the introduction to " Système social ".

etc. Holbach would be very astonished if he were to discover that all this is nothing more than the " surface " of historical phenomena.

For the " philosophers ", history was only the conscious activity of persons (more or less wise and often very unwise). But such a view is very narrow and superficial. In all great historical movements we see people standing at the head of their contemporaries, expressing their tendencies, formulating their desires. Others in exactly the same way are at the head of reaction, wage war on innovations, on new plans and desires. If there only exists in history conscious human activity, then the " great people " are inevitably the cause of historical movement. Religion, manners, customs, the whole character of a people is from this point of view the creation of one or several great persons acting with definite aims. Let us hear for example what Holbach says about the ancient Jews.

Moses led the Jews through the desert; " He taught them blind obedience, he communicated the will of Heaven to them, the wonderful story of their ancestors, the strange ceremonies in dependence upon which the All-Highest placed his favour. In particular he inspired them with a terrible hatred towards the gods of other nations and a refined cruelty towards those who worshipped them; by the help of death and war he made them slaves submissive to his will, ready to be the tool of his passions and to sacrifice themselves to satisfy his ambitious aims,—in a word he made the Jews monsters of madness and savagery. Filling them with this spirit of destruction he pointed out the countries and possessions of their neighbours to them as an inheritance destined for them by God Himself."[1]

From this point of view the history of the Jewish people is no different from the history of other peoples. All peoples have had their Moses, although not such a pernicious one, for, if we believe Holbach and Voltaire, there was no nation in history worse than the Israelites. "Generally all those personalities have emerged from the bosom of civilised nations which have taught to those families and hordes, which were still scattered and not yet united in nations the elements of society, agriculture, the arts, have given them laws, gods, worship, and religious ideas. They softened manners, they brought them together, they taught them to make beneficiary use of their strength, to help one another and to satisfy their needs with the minimum of effort. In this way making their existence happier, they won themselves love and respect, obtained the right to dictate their views, compelled them to accept their opinions which they had invented or borrowed from the civilised countries whence they had come. History shows us the most famous legislators as people possessing a treasure of useful knowledge taken from the civilised peoples and bringing industry, help and the

[1] " Le christianisme dévoilé ", p. 35.

arts to the savage nations to whom they were hitherto unknown. Such people were Bacchus, Orpheus, Triptolemy, etc."[1]

In connection with this view of the origin of civilisation Holbach naturally posed the question as to whether it is possible to think that all modern civilised nations have at some time or other passed through the stage of savagery. This question, however easy for our time, caused no little trouble to our philosophers. He had no definite views on the origin of humanity. How could he therefore argue about primitive social conditions? Perhaps, he says, this was a condition of savagery; but how to explain savagery in itself? Here there comes to his help a new deus ex machina in the shape of the amazing revolutions said to have shaken our globe. It may be, Holbach says, that such revolutions have more than once disposed of the whole human race. People in avoiding their doom were not in a position to preserve for posterity the knowledge and arts which perished with each catastrophe.

So it became possible that people fell many times again into the condition of ignorance after they had already reached a definite level of civilisation. Perhaps the deep ignorance in which humanity finds itself in regard to many of the objects most interesting to it is the consequence of these periodical renewals. Perhaps they are the real source of the inequality of our religious and political institutions. We have already seen that

[1] " Système de la Nature ", p. 25.

humanity, according to Holbach, is unable to know whether the animal came before the egg or vice versa. Now it appears that Holbach did not know whether civilisation came before savagery or the contrary.

Holbach was satisfied with the knowledge that " the human race became unhappy through error " and that it is necessary to free humanity from error. He spared neither labour nor money to fulfil this noble task. Holbach consecrated his whole life to the struggle against " prejudices." He considered religion the most deeply rooted prejudice and fought against it unceasingly. Voltaire in his fight against the " infamous " Church did not encroach upon " the supreme being ", but only tried to reason with him. Voltaire was in religion, so to say, a constitutionalist. He wished to limit the all-powerfulness of " the supreme being " by the laws of nature in the edition thought out by the " philosophers ".

But the French materialists were warm Republicans in heavenly affairs. They guillotined God long before the invention of the good Doctor Guillotine. They hated him like a personal enemy. A capricious, vengeful and harsh despot, like the Judaic Jehovah, he outraged all their best sentiments both as citizens and as human beings. And they rose in revolt against this harsh domination, rose in passionate revolt, exactly as though they were the oppressed victims of a superior power.

" It is impossible to love a being the idea of which

evokes nothing but horror," exclaims Holbach. " . . . How can one look without fear on a god whom you know to be barbarian enough to curse you? No person can have even a spark of love for a god who for ninety-nine out of every hundred of his children has prepared eternal and frightful tortures . . . And you, Messieurs the theologians, must come to the conclusion that, in accordance with your principles, this god is infinitely worse than the worst of humans."[1]

The English materialists who were Holbach's contemporaries were on a friendly footing with the Judaic God. They felt towards him only " feelings of love and respect ". They lived in different social conditions. Two bodies that consist of the same elements, but taken in different proportions, possess different chemical qualities. More than this. Yellow phosphorus is very different from red. Chemists are not astonished at this. They say that this depends upon the difference in the molecular structure of these elements. And at the same time they are always astonished when they observe that the same ideas assume a different colour and lead to different practical results in different countries with almost the same social structure. The movement of ideas is only the expression of a social movement, and the different paths which the latter makes for itself, the different attacks to which it is continually subjected, exactly correspond to the different groupings of social forces. The

[1] " Le bon sens puisé dans la nature ", I, p. 89-93.

character of thought always depends on the character of being.[1]

" It will hardly be disputed," wrote the English materialist Priestley, " —that the general aim of virtue encounters a practical help from the side of faith in sufficient retribution for all good and evil acts in the future life ".[2] The French deist Voltaire, obliged to him for many things, was of the same opinion. The patriarch of Ferney wrote much that was banal on this question. The French materialist Holbach thought otherwise.

" Almost all men believe in an avenging and rewarding God; however, in every country we find that the number of the wicked greatly exceeds the number of the good. If we wish to seek the true cause of so general a corruption we shall find it in theological ideas themselves, not in the imaginary causes that the different religions of the world have invented to explain human depravity. Men are corrupt because they are almost everywhere badly governed; they are unworthily governed because religion has made their sovereigns

[1] Often the same thought in the mouths of two people who are seeking different practical aims has a completely different sense. According to Holbach true religion in every country is the religion of the executioner. In fact Hobbes says the same. But what a difference in the sense which this idea has for the philosophy of each of them!

[2] " A free discussion of the doctrine of materialism and philosophical necessity, in a correspondence between Dr. Price and Dr. Priestley." London 1778, Introduction, p. viii, ix.

divine; the latter, assured of impunity and themselves perverted, have of necessity made their peoples wretched and wicked. Under the rule of unreasonable masters they have never been guided by reason. Blinded by impostor priests, their reason became useless to them."

It follows that religion and its influence on government are the causes of all evil and form the whole content of history.[1] This, in the real sense of the word, is ' Bossuet reversed '. The author of the ' Discours sur l'histoire universelle ' was convinced that religion arranges everything for the best, while Holbach on the other hand shows that religion arranges everything in the worst possible way. In this difference is comprised the whole progress made in the philosophy of history during the century. Its practical consequences were incalculable, but the understanding of historical facts gained only very little from this.

The philosophers were turning in a vicious circle. On the one hand they conceived of man as the product of social environment. " It is in education we should seek for the chief source of the passions and virtues in man, of the errors or truths which fill his head, of the habits praiseworthy or demanding censure, and of the merits and talents distinguishing him, which have been acquired by man ".[2] On the other hand the source of all social disorders is found in " ignorance of the clearest foundations of politics ". The social

---

[1] " Système de la Nature ", II, p. 219.
[2] " Système social," I, p. 15.

environment is created by " public opinion ", that is by man.

This fundamental contradiction comes up again in various forms in the works of Holbach as, furthermore, it does in the works of all the other " philosophers ".

1. *Man is the product of social environment.* From this it follows logically that the world is not ruled by " public opinion ". Let us listen to Holbach. " People are only what organisation, varied by habit, education, example, government, the permanent or temporary environing conditions, makes them. Their religious ideas and imagined systems must depend on their temperaments, inclinations and interests and be adapted to them." " If we investigate things coolly then it appears that the beliefs of different peoples have only served as the cover for human passions ". " Our environing, momentary interests, deep-rooted habits, public opinion, are much more powerful than imagined beings or than our speculations, since both the one and the other depend upon this organisation ". The power of " speculation " and " imagined beings " is none the less considerable because out of a hundred thousand people hardly two will be found to ask themselves what is God, to question the essence of their beliefs and convictions. People are inspired to activity not by general considerations of reason, but by passions, as Bayle had already declared, and before him Seneca.

2. *Man is the product of social environment.* As for the gods, man created them in his own initial like-

ness. " Man, in bowing down to god bowed down to himself ".[1] (Compare Feuerbach). Surely it is evident that a capricious god, sensitive to praise, always expecting the reverences of his subjects, is created in the image and likeness of the earthly princes?[2]

3. *Man is the product of social environment.* " If we think only a little upon what is being accomplished before our eyes, then we see that the stamp of rule (that is of government; we shall soon see how and why the influence of social environment with the ' philosophers ' was reduced to the influence of government) is observed on everything: on the character, the opinions, the laws, the customs, the education and the manners of a nation ".[3] " So, only the vices of society make its members vicious. Then man becomes a wolf before his fellows ".[4]

The other side of the antinomy:

1. *Social environment is created by " public opinion ", i.e. by human beings.* " Hence it follows

[1] " Le bon sens ", I, p. 57.

[2] " Christianisme dévoilé ", p. 176.

[3] " Système social ", III, p. 5. Grimm went even further in this direction. " The influence of the boldest opinions," he says, " is equal to nothing. Not a single book is able to corrupt morals and, unfortunately, not a single philosopher can improve them. Only the government and legislation have this power. In accordance with their interference the level of public morality is lowered or highered and books are here absolutely powerless ". (" Correspondance littéraire," Janvier 1772.)

[4] " Politique naturelle ", I, p. 11-12.

quite logically that public opinion rules the world and that the human race has become unhappy in consequence of ' error '." " If we consult experience," says Holbach, " we shall see that it is in illusions and sacred opinions that we should seek the real source of this endless evil with which everywhere we see the human race overwhelmed. The ignorance of natural causes created the gods. Imposture made them terrible. Their harmful idea pursued man without making him better, made him tremble fruitlessly, filled his spirit with chimeras, was opposed to the progress of reason, prevented him from seeking happiness. His fears made him the slave of those who deceived him under the pretext of doing him good; he did evil when he was told that his gods demanded crimes of him; he lived in misfortune because he was made to understand that the gods condemned him to be wretched; he never dared to resist his god or free himself from his fetters because he was made to understand that stupidity, renunciation of reason, dullness of spirit, abjection of soul, were the sure means of winning eternal happiness ".[1]

2. *Social environment is created by " public*

[1] " Système de la Nature ", I, p. 290-291. Suard in his turn, defines public opinion as follows: " I understand by public opinion the result of the truths and errors distributed in a given nation, the result determining their judgement of merit or contempt, of love or hate and forming their inclinations and habits, vices and virtues, in a word—their morals. It is necessary to say that opinion rules over the world."

opinion" i.e. by human beings. "Madness consecrated by heaven was necessary to compel a freedom-
loving being constantly striving for happiness to believe
that the bearers of public authority had received from
the gods the right to make slaves and beggars of man.
Religions were necessary to picture divinity in the
image of a tyrant in order to compel people to believe
that unjust tyrants represent this divinity on earth ".[1]

3. *Social environment is created by "public
opinion" i.e. by human beings.* "How do once
noble nations find themselves to-day under the shame-
ful yoke of degrading despotism? Because public
opinion has changed in them. . . . Because superstition, the ally of tyranny, has succeeded in corrupting their minds and making them cowardly and insensitive. . . . How have whole nations become drunk
with commerce and greed of riches? Because public
opinion has convinced them that only money brings
real happiness, whereas in fact it is only the deceptive
substitute of riches and does not bring even the slightest
benefit to the public well-being ".[2] "The nations,"
says Holbach, "did not know the true foundations of
authority; they did not dare to demand happiness from
the kings who had been charged to procure it for them;
they believed that sovereigns, decked out as gods,
received at birth the right to command the rest of
mortals, could dispose at their will of the happiness of

[1] "Politique naturelle ", II, p. 11.
[2] "Système social ", III, p. 9-10.

peoples and are not to be held to account for the unfortunates whom they made. As the necessary consequence of these opinions, politics degenerated into the fatal art of sacrificing the happiness of all to the caprice of one or of a few privileged scoundrels."[1]

We know that it is " not given " to man to know whether the animal appeared before the egg or the egg before the animal. Neither was it given to the materialists of the 18th century to know whether " public opinion " forms the social environment or the social environment forms " public opinion ". Indeed for him who is incapable of departing from the metaphysical point of view there is nothing more difficult than to answer this question.

If, as Locke argued, there exist no innate principles; if, as the materialists of the 18th century declared, man is only a " sensitive " being; if sensations produce in him ideas as " the images, traces, impressions, received by our senses "; if, finally, man is no more free in his thoughts than in his acts, then it is very strange to seek " in the opinions " of people the secret of this or that human action. For from the point of view brought forward our ideas are only what the impressions received by us make them. But such impressions are left not only by " nature " in the real sense of the word. From birth social environment takes possession of a man and forms his brain, which is only " the soft wax suitable for the reception of all

[1] " Système de la Nature ", I, p. 291.

impressions ".[1] So, in desiring to understand the history of " public opinion " we must give ourselves an exact account of the history of social environment, that is of the development of society. This is the inevitable conclusion to which sensualist materialism came. The famous statue invented by Condillac could only reach a position of rest after it had succeeded in explaining the change in its " opinions " by means of the change in social relations, that is the relations towards " its own like ".

So we must turn to history. But the " philosophers ", seeing in history merely the conscious activity of humanity, could find in it nothing beyond " the opinions of man ".

And so they met with an antinomy: opinion is the consequence of social environment, and, on the contrary, opinion is the cause of this or that quality of the environment. And this antinomy was all the more bound to confuse the ideas of the philosophers since the conception of cause and effect, at least in regard to social life, was for them, as for all metaphysicians, firm, immobile, and, so to say, fosillised. It is only as a metaphysician that Grimm could say that " the influence of opinions is equal to nothing ".

The highest, most philosophical point of view to which the metaphysicians could attain was the conception of reciprocity between the different aspects of social life. This is the point of view of Montesquieu.

[1] " Le bon sens ", I, p. 32.

But reciprocity or " the nearest truth of the relations between effect and cause ", as Hegel defines it, explains absolutely nothing of the historical process. " If we get no further than studying a given content under the point of view of reciprocity, we are taking up an attitude which leaves matters utterly incomprehensible. We are left with a mere dry fact; and the call for mediation, which is the chief motive in applying the relation of causality, is still unanswered ".[1]   However, much more unpleasant things happen than are here shown by Hegel.

Man is the product of social environment.   The character of this environment is, by hypothesis, determined by the action of the " government ". The actions of the government, for example legislative activity, belong to the sphere of conscious human activity.   This conscious activity in its turn, depends on the " opinions " of the persons acting. . . . Unnoticed one of the sides of the antinomy has turned into its opposite.   The difficulty is evidently set aside and the " philosopher " continues his " investigations " with quiet conscience.   The point of view of " reciprocity " was abandoned as soon as it had been reached.

This is not all.   The apparent solution of the antinomy is simply a complete break with materialism. The human brain, that " soft wax " which assumes different forms under the influence of impressions coming from the social environment, is finally trans-

[1] " Encyklopädie ", I, Teil, p. 155-156.

formed into the creator of this environment to which it was obliged for its impressions. Not knowing what comes next, materialist sensualism is forced to go backwards again.

The author of the " System of Nature " assures us that it is very easy to recognise the influence of government on character, opinions, laws, habits, etc. Government, consequently, has influence upon laws. This is very simple and perfectly evident, but it merely means that the civil law of a nation has as its historical source the public law of the same nation. One law depends on another, " laws " on " laws ". The antinomy disappears, but only because one side of it, the one which should have formulated the final conclusion of materialist sensualism was in reality merely a trivial tautology.

A real overcoming of the difficulty encountered by this materialism called for two conditions :

1. It was necessary to renounce the metaphysical outlook which excluded any idea of evolution and deplorably confused the logical conceptions of the " philosophers ". Only on this condition could it " be granted " to them to recognise which came first in both natural science and social science : did the animal come from the egg or the egg from the animal.

2. The necessary conviction had to be reached that that " human nature " with which the materialists of the 18th century have dealt explains absolutely nothing in the historical development of humanity. It was

necessary to make one step further, to rise above the natural-historical outlook and actually to stand upon the ground of social science. It was necessary to understand that social environment has its own laws of development in no wise dependent upon man looked upon as a " feeling, understanding and reasonable being ", but, on the contrary, having a decisive influence on his feelings, ideas and judgements.

We shall see how dialectical materialism solved this task in the 19th century. But before speaking of its brilliant discoveries we will explain the views of the man who more than any other by his example and fearless logic exposed the complete insufficiency and limitation of metaphysical materialism. This man was Helvétius.

HELVETIUS

HELVETIUS

" TO Helvétius, the elegant farmer general and honourable gentleman, the unselfish benefactor whom Voltaire in the full flattery of historical reminiscence nick-named the Athenian, there came the idea of writing a book. To accomplish this, at the conversations with the philosophers whom he invited to dinner, he collected their theories, views and paradoxes. By artificially exciting interesting arguments he succeeded in arousing the fiery temperament of Diderot, the wit of Suard, the amusing and caustic humour of the Abbé Galiani. Then, whilst conscientiously expounding them, he brought their views together into a compact theory. The result of these conversations which he had heard, collected and analysed, was the book ' De L'Esprit' (' On the Spirit '), that is materialism in metaphysics, personal interest in morality ".[1]

The reader now knows how the chief work of

[1] Demogeot, " Histoire de la littérature française depuis ses origines jusqu'à nos jours," 22—e éd., Paris 1886, p. 493. This book is part of the " Histoire universelle ", published by a group of professors under the editorship of V. Duruy.

Helvétius was born. In this instance the chatter-box Demogeot is only repeating the fable which for more than a century now has been passed on from one literary scandal-monger to another. Demogeot was a kindly gossip. He says nothing bad about Helvétius, he allows the reader to suspect evil. There are less kindly but franker gossipers. They tell the reader that the chief motive inspiring our philosopher in his investigations was unlimited vanity. To this vanity we are obliged for the " sophisms " of Helvétius. It prevented him from creating anything firm and sound. Gossipers are always and everywhere distinguished by extreme wit. They are just the people for writing literary and political history. In their historical writings everything is clear and comprehensible. They can be read with great pleasure, with small effort and immense benefit. They are preferable to the kind of writer, who, like good old Hegel, for example, saw something more than gossip in history. Such writers are pretty dull company, but . . . *audiatur et altera pars* (let the other side be heard).

In speaking of the role of great men in history Hegel thunders against " petty humanising, which instead of making the general and essential features of human nature the object of study, is chiefly occupied with the partial and accidental, with separate motives and passions, etc." In his opinion, " great men desired what they did, and did what they desired ". The same, of course, can be said, only " in rather different words ", of all those who in one sphere or another, with greater or less success, have worked for the good of humanity as they understood it. It might be said that the " point of view of envy " abhorred by Hegel brings us no further forward in the comprehension and estimation of different historical epochs. It might be said . . . yes, a great deal might be said, but will it be listened to? The gossipers are much more readily heard. They, for example, say that Helvétius was a dangerous sophist, vain and superficial, and with this they remain very satisfied with themselves, with their wit and honesty, and . . . the verdict is ready.

German historians in particular treat Helvétius in this fashion. In France, at least, justice is paid to his personal worth.[1] In Germany they avoid risky condescension with regard to such a " dangerous " person. In Germany they have disparaged Helvétius even more than Lamettrie. Though the latter was no less " dangerous," his late majesty, Frederick the Great, was kind enough to say a few pleasant words about him after his death. But *voluntas regis suprema lex* (the will of the sovereign is the supreme law), and German learned men know this law better than any other precisely because they are learned.

[1] " How necessary it is to be cautious of illusion in search of a system is clear from the example of Helvétius. He had virtues, but his book is the negation of all virtue " (La Harpe, " Réfutation du livre de l'Esprit, prononcée au Lycée Républican dans les séances du 26 et 29 Mars et du 3 et 5 Avril ", Paris, an 5, 1797, p. 54).

An astonishing fact! Although the theories of Helvétius frightened even the " philosophers " and among his opponents there were such men as Diderot, nevertheless in France he was the object of controversy much more after the Revolution than before it. La Harpe recognises that his refutation of the " sophisms " of this man in 1788 did not in general produce such an impression as nine years later in 1797. Then, says La Harpe, they understood that materialist philosophy was a " militant doctrine ", a revolutionary doctrine. In 1797 the bourgeoisie was no longer in any need of such theories which had begun to be a prolonged threat to its new attainments. It was necessary to have done with materialism and they finished with it without asking whether the arguments of sycophants like La Harpe were really as well founded as they appeared. Other times, other desires, other desires, other philosophies.[1]

---

[1] Marat also did not like Helvétius. This philosopher for him was merely " a corrupt and superficial mind ", his " systems " absurd, his book a " constant network of sophisms carefully decked out with great learning ". (" De l'homme ou des principes et des lois de l'influence de l'âme sur le corps et du corps sur l'âme," par J. P. Marat, docteur en médecine, Amsterdam 1775, p. xv-xvi, du Discours préliminaire.) But this book of Marat belongs to the pre-revolutionary period of his life. Moreover, the opinions of revolutionaries are not always revolutionary opinions. According to Marat, " both men and animals consist of two different substances—soul and body " . . . " eternal wisdom " placed the soul in the brain envelope (!). The nerve fluid is the place where both these substances are in communication. " In mechanical movements

As for the gossipers, they have a sound reason to complain of Helvétius. They rarely understand him, and not only because his ideas surpass the limits of their horizon. Helvétius possessed an original way of expounding his theories which was bound to embarrass the gossipers. Less than any other of the writers of his time did he respect what Nordau calls the conditioned lie. As a man of the world and a subtle observer he knew French " society " in the 18th century perfectly. A caustic and satirical writer, he never missed a chance of telling truths to that society which were not easy for it to digest and had nothing in common with those harmless truths which are always so easy to utter. Hence an endless number of misunderstandings. What he said about his contemporaries they have taken for his ideal. Madame de Boufflers said of him that he exposed everybody's secret. She thought that it was just this which gave value and importance to the book " On the Spirit ". This *quid pro quo* brought with it another consequence. Speaking of the respect due to " virtue " Helvétius says that in " despotic states " it is looked on with contempt and only its name is respected. " Although they constantly invoke virtue and demand it from citizens they behave the chief motive force is nerve fluid. In arbitrary movements it is subordinate to the soul and is the means which it makes use of in order to inspire them " (I, p. 24-40, 107). This is all amazingly trivial. In his manner of treating his predecessors and in his susceptible vanity Marat is very like Dühring.

83

towards it as though it were a truth obtained on condition that they have enough sense to keep quiet about it ". This statement wins the approval of Madame de Boufflers. She declares it to be true, witty and delightful. She declares that the secret of every man is here exposed. Helvétius continues. He explains why things take place as he says. He shows how in despotic states peoples' interests force them to hate " virtue ". Madame de Boufflers continues to agree. But then there enters the discussion a certain Lampe, generally appearing as a German, but sometimes as a Frenchman, and he in his turn lifts his voice, saying that Helvétius praises contempt for virtue. When the conversation turns to love, Helvétius says that wherever " the rich and strong " do not take any part in government they should give themselves up to love as the truest cure for boredom. Madame de Boufflers smiles roguishly; the amiable blue stocking knows this better than the philosopher. But the philosopher does not stop at this. He asks himself how love can become a permanent occupation and answers that " love is surrounded by dangers, the lover must all the time endeavour to outwit jealousy, which is watchful and hinders his plans ". He comes to the conclusion that in such conditions " the coquette is a ravishing mistress ". As before Madame de Boufflers agrees. But now there comes on the scene a Madame Buchholz and, pale with anger, accuses our philosopher of encouraging coquetry and attacking female virtue, the well tried virtue of Madame Buchholz, etc. And this objection endlessly repeated becomes evermore deeply fixed in peoples' minds. The misunderstanding has been kept up in our own day and has taken firm root in the heads of those who have never read Helvétius. In any case, to read Helvétius with the eyes of a Madame Buchholz could hardly make any difference in this respect, for the lady is very shortsighted, for all her virtue and respectability.

Was Helvétius what may be called a materialist in the strict sense of the word? Thanks to his reputation this is very often doubted. " The reasonable and restrained Buffon, the discreet and diplomatic Grimm, the vain and superficial Helvétius," said the late Lange " all approach closely to materialism, although they do not give us that firm outlook and those consistent conclusions from sound ideas by which Lamettrie, for all the lightness of his expressions, was distinguished ".[1] The French echo of the German Neokantian, Jules Soury, repeats this opinion word for word.[2]

We want to examine the question for ourselves.

The question as to whether there exists in man an immaterial substance to which he owes his psychic life does not enter into the sphere of Helvétius' investigations. He only touches on this question by the way

[1] " Geschichte des Materialismus," 2 Aufl., Iserlon 1873, I, p. 360.
[2] " Bréviaire de l'histoire du matérialisme ", Paris 1883, p. 645-646.

and examines it with the greatest caution. On the one hand, he tries not to annoy the censor. For this reason he speaks with obvious respect of the Church which has " established our faith on this point ". On the other hand, he does not like philosophical " fantasies ". We should go along the path of observation, he says, halting the moment it halts us and have the courage not to know what it is still impossible to know. This sounds rather " restrained " than " vain " or " superficial ". Lange would have felt this and pointed it out if it had been a question of a less " dangerous " writer. But since he is talking of Helvétius, he finds another measure and another scale. It appeared obvious to him that the " vain and superficial " author of the book " On the Spirit " could only be " vain and superficial ".[1] In all the main questions of " metaphysics " (for example in the questions of matter, space, infinity, etc.) Helvétius in fact shared the views of the English materialist John Toland. To be convinced of this it is sufficient to compare " The Letters to Serena " (London 1704) of the latter with the fourth chapter

[1] In the opinion of Helvétius only our own existence is evident for us. On the contrary the existence of other bodies is only a probability, " a probability which is undoubtedly very great and in practical life is equal to palpability, but which is nevertheless only probability ". Anybody else who had expressed something like this Lange would have placed with the crowd of " critical minds ". But no kind of " criticism " was able to rehabilitate Helvétius and to remove the blot of " superficiality " from him which above all impressed the sight of the sound historian of materialism.

of the first part of the book "On the Spirit". For Lange, Toland without any doubt was an outstanding materialist. His ideas appeared to him as clear, in so far as that is possible. As for Helvétius, he merely "approached" materialism since his superficiality prevented him from firmly holding to one main idea. "So history is written". How fatal is the influence of "superficial" persons! The "soundest" people through reading the latter become in their turn superficial!

"Does matter possess the capacity of sensation?" "Always and from all sides it has been maintained that matter felt or did not feel and on this subject there have been very long and very vague disputes. Only very late have people arrived at the point of asking what the dispute was about and of fixing a precise idea for this word matter. If its meaning had been fixed at first, it would have been recognised that men are, so to say, the creators of matter, that matter is not a being, that in nature there are only individuals to which the name of body has been given and that it is only possible to understand by this word matter the collection of properties common to all these bodies. Once the meaning of this word had been determined in this way, it only remained to know whether space, solidity, impenetrability were the only properties common to all bodies; and whether the discovery of a force such as attraction, for example, could not make one suspect that bodies had some other unknown properties such

87

as the faculty of sensation which, only manifesting itself in the organised bodies of animals, might however be common to all individuals. The question reduced to this point, it would have been felt that if it is strictly impossible to show that all bodies are absolutely insensible, any man who is not on this subject enlightened by revelation can only decide the question by calculating and comparing the probability of this opinion with the probability of the contrary opinion. To put an end to this dispute it was not therefore necessary to construct different systems of the world, to lose oneself in the combination of possibilities and to make those prodigious efforts of mind which have only ended and should really only have ended in more or less ingenious errors."[1] This long quotation shows however both the kinship of Helvétius' materialism with Toland's materialism[2] and the character of

[1] " De l'Esprit ", discours I, ch. IV.

[2] Evidently this kinship explains why the book " Les progrès de la raison dans la recherche du vrai," printed in the Paris edition of his works is attributed to Helvétius. There is not a single original page in this book. It is a translation of one part of the " Letters to Serena " of Toland to which a few extracts from the " System of Nature " have been added as well as from some of the more or less well-known books of the period. It is all very badly put together and badly understood by an unknown " author ". Helvétius could have had nothing to do with such a product. Yet another book exists attributed to him : " Le vrai sens du Système de la Nature ". It may be his, but we know nothing positive in this respect and shall be the less inclined to make use of it in our quota-

what it was desired to call the scepticism or probabilism of Helvétius. But in his opinion it is not the materialists but the idealists of different schools who are taken up with " philosophic fantasies ". He recommends them to be prudent, careful, and to take account of probabilities. This prudence, this care should show them that at the basis of their negation of the sensitivity of matter lies their imagination, that not the qualities of " bodies " but only the definition which they give of matter, that is, exclusively the word, prevent them from uniting the concept of the body with the capacity for sensation. Scepticism is here a weapon directed solely against the adversaries of materialism. It is exactly the same where Helvétius speaks about " the existence of bodies ". The capacity of matter for sensation is only a probability! Perfectly true. But what does this prove against the materialist? For in its turn, the very existence of bodies is only a probability, and, moreover, it would be stupid to deny it. In this way Helvétius developed his argument and if it proves anything, then it is first of all that he did not stand still before his sceptical doubt.

Helvétius knew, just as well as did all his contemporaries, that we know bodies only through the sensations which they excite in us. This shows once again that Lange was mistaken in declaring that " materialism obstinately accepts the world of sensual

tions since it adds nothing to what may be found in his books " De l'Esprit " and " De l'Homme ."

phenomena for the world of real things ".[1] But this did not prevent Helvétius from being a convinced materialist. He quotes a " famous English chemist " whose opinion on the sensitivity of matter he clearly shares. Here are the words of this chemist: " Two kinds of properties are recognised in bodies, of which some are permanent and unchangeable: such are, impenetrability, weight, mobility, etc. These qualities belong to Physics in general.

" These same bodies have other qualities the existence of which is fugitive and transient, is in turn produced and destroyed by certain combinations, analyses, or movements in the internal parts. These kinds of properties form the different branches of Natural History, of Chemistry, etc. and belong to particular branches of Physics.

" Iron for example, is a compound of Phlogiston and a certain earth. In this form of composition it is amenable to the power of attraction of loadstone. But if the iron is decomposed this property is destroyed. Loadstone has no action upon an iron soil deprived of its Phlogiston. . . .

[1] " Geschichte des Materialismus ", I, p. 378. It is astonishing that Lange finds an " element " of Kantian teaching in Robinet. For Robinet says of the thing in itself only what Holbach and Helvétius said. It is no less astonishing that Lange places the author of the book " De la Nature " among the materialists, although Helvétius, in his opinion, only approximates to them. Lange is guided all the time by a strange criterion!

" Now why should not organisations in the animal Kingdom also produce this singular quality which we call the faculty of feeling? Every phenomenon of medicine and history proves that this power in animals is only the result of the structure of their bodies, that this power begins with the formation of their organs, is preserved as long as they exist, and is lost at last by the dissolution of these organs.

" If the metaphysicians ask me what becomes of the animal's faculty of sensation, I shall answer them that the same thing becomes of it as becomes of the property of iron of being attracted by loadstone."[1]   Helvétius

---

[1] Quoted from the book " De l'Homme ", Section II, Chap. II. In the 1773 edition of this work it is stated that the quotation is borrowed from the " Treatise on the Principles of Chemistry ". We have been unable to find this book. We can, however, quote what Priestley says in his dispute with Price: " To make my meaning, if possible, better understood, I will use the following comparisons. The power of cutting in a razor, depends upon a certain cohesion, and arrangement of the parts of which it consists. If we suppose this razor to be dissolved in any acid liquor, its power of cutting is certain to be lost, or cease to be, though no particle of the metal that constituted the razor be annihilated by the process; and its former shape, and power of cutting, etc., may be restored to it after the metal has been precipitated. Thus when the body is dissolved by putric action, its power of thinking entirely ceases." (" A free discussion of the doctrine of materialism, etc.," London 1778, p. 82-83.) This is also the point of view of the chemist quoted by Helvétius. In the given circumstances we are in no way interested by the religious ideas which Priestley managed to reconcile with his materialism. Neither

was not only a materialist but among his contemporaries he maintained the main ideas of his materialism with the greatest " consistency ". He was so " consistent " that he horrified the other materialists. Not one of them was bold enough to follow him in his daring conclusions. In this sense he did actually only stand near to people like Holbach, since these people were only able to approximate to him.

Our soul is only the capacity for sensation. Reason is only the activity of this capacity. In man everything is sensation: " Physical sensibility is consequently the principle of his needs, of his passions, of his sociability, of his ideas, of his judgements, of his wills, of his actions. . . . Man is a machine which, put into motion by physical sensibility, must do everything which it demands ".[1] Thus the starting point of Helvétius is absolutely identical with the starting point of Holbach. This is the foundation upon which our " dangerous sophist " built. Let us now examine

is there any necessity to emphasise that the views of the materialists of the last century upon chemistry are not the views of our time.

[1] " De l'Homme ", Section II, Chap. X. Helvétius understands perfectly that we are to a great extent made by memory, but the organ of memory, he says, is purely physical and its function consists in giving life to our past impressions. It should therefore call forth real sensations in us; in this way everything is brought down to the capacity of sensation; everything in man is sensation.

more closely what there is original in the architecture of his building.

What is virtue? In the 18th century, there was no philosopher who did not discuss this question in his own way. For Helvétius the matter was perfectly simple. Virtue consists in the knowledge of what is due from people to one another. Its premise consequently is the education of society. "Born on a desert island, left to myself, I live without vice and without virtue. I can show neither the one nor the other. What must I understand then by these words virtuous and vicious? Actions which are useful or harmful to society. To my mind this simple and clear idea is to be preferred to any obscure and high-sounding declamation upon virtue ".[1]

The general interest is the measure and foundation of virtue. Therefore the more harmful to society our acts are, the more vicious they are. The more advantageous to society they are, the more virtuous they are. *Salus populi suprema lex* (the good of the people is the highest law). The " virtue " of our philosopher is in the first place political virtue. The preaching of morality leads to nothing: preaching has never yet made a single hero. We must give to society an organisation able to teach its members respect for the common interest. The corruption of morals merely means the separation of public and private interest.

---

[1] Ibid., II, Chap. XVI, the last note to this Chapter.

The best preacher of morality is the legislator who has succeeded in destroying this separation.

We often meet with the statement that J. S. Mill's " Utilitarianism " as a teaching on morality greatly surpasses the ethic of the materialists of the 18th century, since the latter wished to make personal interest the foundation of morality, whilst the English philosopher placed the principle of the greatest happiness of the greatest number in the first place. The reader now sees that in this respect the merits of J. S. Mill are more than doubtful. The happiness of the greatest number is merely a very weak copy, deprived of its revolutionary colouring, of the " general interest " of the French materialists. But if this is the case then whence comes the opinion which perceives in J. S. Mill's " Utilitarianism " a happy variation upon the 18th century materialist teaching upon morality?

What is the principle of the greatest happiness of the greatest number? It is the sanction for human action. In this respect the materialists have nothing to learn from Mill's famous book. But the materialists were not satisfied with seeking for sanctions. Before them was the task of solving a scientific problem. In what way does Man, since he is only sensation, learn to value the common good? By what miracle does he forget the demands of his physical sensations and arrive at aims which have nothing in common with the latter? In the sphere and within the limits of this problem the materialists actually did take personal interest as their starting point. But to take personal interest as the starting point only means to repeat once more the argument that man is a feeling being and nothing but a feeling being. Thus personal interest for the materialists was not a moral homily but simply a scientific fact.[1]

Holbach got round the difficulty of this problem by means of wordy terminology. " When we say that interest is the only motive of human actions we wish by this to indicate that every man works after his own fashion for his own happiness which he places in some visible or hidden object, whether real or imaginary, and towards obtaining which the whole system of his conduct is directed ".[2] In other words this means that it is impossible to reduce personal interest simply to the demand of " physical sensations ". But at the same time, for Holbach, as for all the materialists of the 18th century, man is only sensation. Here is a logical jump and thanks to this logical jump Holbach's " Ethics " inspire the historians of philosophy with less disgust than the ethics of Helvétius. In Lange's opinion

[1] Charles Darwin understood splendidly what the moral philosophers only rarely understand. " The philosophers . . . formerly agreed that morality is based upon a kind of egoism, but now the principle of the greatest happiness has recently been brought forward. It would however be more correct to take this latter principle as being rather the measure than the motive of behaviour " (" The Origin of Species ").

[2] " Système de la Nature ", London 1781, I, p. 268.

" Holbach's ethics are serious and pure ".[1] Hettner, on his side, sees in them something distinct from the ethics of Helvétius.[2]

The author of the book " On the Spirit " was the only philosopher of the 18th century who dared to touch on the question of the origin of moral feelings. He was the only one who dared to deduce them from the " physical sensations " of people.

Man is sensitive to physical satisfaction and to physical suffering. He avoids the second and aims at the first. This constant and inevitable striving is called self-love. This self-love is inseparable from man. It is his chief sensation. " Of all sentiments it is the only one of its kind. To it we owe all our desires, all our passions. They can but be the application of the sentiment of self-love to this or that object." . . . " If you open the book of history you will see that in every country where certain virtues were encouraged by the hope of sensual pleasures, these virtues have been the most common and have enjoyed the greatest renown."[3] The nations which devoted themselves most of all to love were the most manly. " For in these countries women showed favour only to the brave." With the Samnites the greatest beauty was

---

[1] " Geschichte des Materialismus ", I, p. 363.

[2] " Literaturgeschichte des XVIII Jahrhunderts ", Braunschweig 1881, Vol. II, p. 398.

[3] " De l'Homme ", Section IV, Chap. IV : " De l'Esprit ", discours III, Chap. XV.

the reward for the highest military virtue. In Sparta the wise Lycurgus, convinced that " pleasure is the only general motive of man ", succeeded in making love the incentive to bravery. On the principal holidays young, half-naked and beautiful Lacedaemonian girls came out to dance in the popular assemblies. In their songs they insulted the cowards and praised the brave. Only the brave might make demands upon the favours of the fair sex. The Spartans therefore tried to be brave. The passion of love inflamed the passion for glory in their hearts. But the limits of the possible were still not reached in the " wise " institutions of Lycurgus. " Let us suppose, to prove it, that . . . after the example of the virgins consecrated to Isis or to Vesta, the most beautiful Lacedaemonians were consecrated to virtue; that, showing themselves naked in the assembly they were carried off by the warriors as the reward of their courage; and that these young heroes experienced at the same moment the double intoxication of love and of glory; however strange and alien from our morals this legislation may be it is certain that it still made the Spartans more virtuous and more brave, since the force of virtue is always in proportion to the degree of pleasure assigned to it as a reward ".

Helvétius speaks of a double intoxication, of love and of glory. This must not be wrongly understood. In " the passion " of the thirst for glory everything can be reduced to physical sensation. We love glory, like wealth, for the sake of the power which it brings. But what is power? It is the means of compelling others to serve our happiness. But happiness can, in reality, be reduced to physical pleasure. Man is only sensation. All such passions as, for example, the passion for glory, power, wealth, etc., are only artificial passions which may be deduced from physical needs. In order the better to understand this truth it is always necessary to remember that our sensual pleasures and sufferings are of a double kind: real pleasures or sufferings and those which are foreseen. I experience hunger and feel a real suffering. I foresee that I shall die from hunger: I experience a suffering which is foreseen. "When a man who loves beautiful slaves and fine pictures discovers a treasure he is in transports. However, it may be objected that from this he never experiences physical pleasure. I am in agreement with this. But at this moment he obtains the means for securing the objects of his desires. The foresight of approaching pleasure is already a pleasure." It follows of itself that foresight in no wise contradicts the starting point of Helvétius. Foresight represents the consequence of recollection. If I foresee that an insufficiency of food will bring me suffering that proceeds from the fact that I had already once experienced a similar suffering. But recollection is the property of "to a certain degree producing the same effect upon our organs" as suffering or pleasure themselves cause. It is therefore obvious that " all impressions which are called inner sufferings or pleasures are in exactly the same way physical sensations and that the words inner and outer can only be applied to such impressions as are evoked by recollection or the presence of definite objects ".

Foresight, that is physical sensation, compels me to mourn the death of my friend. By his conversation he banished my boredom, " that suffering of the soul which is a purely physical pain "; he would have given his life and fortune in order to save me from death or suffering, by means of all kinds of satisfactions he always strove to increase my pleasure. By the death of my friend a means of pleasure has been taken from me and this brings tears to my eyes. " Delve into the depths of the heart and in all these feelings you will only observe the development of physical satisfaction and physical pain ".

However, your friend, it might be objected against Helvétius, was ready to give up his life and fortune in order to preserve you from suffering. Consequently you yourself acknowledge by this that people do exist who for the sake of achieving an ideal aim are capable of not hearing the voice of your " physical sensation ".

Our philosopher gives no direct answer to this objection. But it is not hard to understand that it should not embarrass him. What, he might ask, is the motive force of heroic acts? The hope of reward. In such acts a man encounters many dangers, but the greater the danger the greater the reward. Interest (physical sensation) prompts that the game is worth the gamble. If this is how things stand with great and famous historical actions then in the self-sacrifice of a friend there is nothing of particular note.

There are people who love science, who lose their health over books and put up with all kinds of hardships in order to obtain knowledge. One might say that love of science has nothing in common with physical pleasure, but this statement would be a mistake. Why does the miser to-day renounce the most essential things? Because he wishes to increase his means of treasure for to-morrow, for the day after to-morrow, in a word, for the future. Splendid. Let us suppose that something similar takes place with the man of learning also and we shall have the solution of the puzzle. " Does the miser desire a fine castle and the man of talent a beautiful woman? If, in order to obtain the one or the other, great wealth and a great reputation are needed, these two men will each work for the increase, the one of his treasure, the other of his renown. But during the time they have spent in acquiring this money and this renown, if they have grown old, if they have contracted habits which they cannot break without an effort of which age has made them incapable, both the miser and the man of talent will die, the one without his castle, the other without his mistress ".[1]

All this is already enough to excite the indignation

[1] " De l'Homme ", Section II, Chap. X.

of " respectable people " throughout the world and to make it clear how and why Helvétius got his bad reputation. But it is also sufficient to show the weak side of his " analysis ". Let us add one more quotation to those we have so far made.

" While recognising that our passions originally have their source in physical sensibility, one might still believe that in the actual conditions in which civilised nations exist, these passions exist independently of the causes which produce them. I am going then, by tracing the metamorphosis of physical pains and pleasures into artificial pains and pleasures, to show that in passions such as avarice, ambition, pride and friendship, the object of which appears least of all to belong to the pleasures of the senses, it is nevertheless always physical pain and pleasure which we evade or seek ".[1]

Thus there is no heredity. According to Darwin the intellectual and moral properties of man are variable; "And we have every ground for believing that the variations have the property of hereditary transmission ".[2] According to Helvétius man's capacities are extremely variable, but the variations are not transmitted from one generation to another, since their basis, the capacity for physical sensation, remains unchanged. Helvétius was sufficiently pene- trating to perceive the phenomena of evolution. He

[1] " De l'Esprit ", discours III, Chap. IX.
[2] " The Origin of Man ".

sees that "One and the same race of animals, independently of the character and abundance of its food, becomes stronger or weaker, develops or falls back ". He also notices that the same thing is applicable to oak trees. "We see small, large, straight, crooked oaks and not one of them is absolutely like the other ". On what does this depend? "Perhaps on the fact that not one of them receives the same culture from the other, does not grow in the same place, is not exposed to the actions of one and the same wind and is not sown in the same soil? " This is a perfectly logical explanation. But Helvétius does not stop here.

He asks the question: "Does the difference in different substances lie in their germs or in their development? " This is not the question of an idle mind. But mark the sense of the dilemma: either in the germs, or in their development. Our philosopher does not even suspect that the history of the species may leave its traces in the structure of the germ. The history of a species? For him, as for his contemporaries, it does not exist at all. He only takes into account the individual. He is only interested in individual "nature", he only observes individual "development". We are far from being satisfied by Darwin's theory of the inheritance of moral and intellectual "characteristics.". It is only the first word in evolutionary science. But we know very well that whatever results the latter may bring us to, it will be

successful only through the application of the dialectical
method to the study of phenomena, which are by
nature dialectical in their very essence. Helvétius
remains a metaphysician even when his instincts impel
him to another and completely opposite point of view,
to the dialectical point of view.

He recognises that he " knows nothing " as to
whether the difference in beings lies exclusively in
their (individual) development. Such a hypothesis
seems overbold to him. And in fact there would
follow from it what Lucretius, who was well known
to the materialist " philosophers ", considered the
greatest absurdity :

> . . . Ex omnibus rebus
> Omne genus nasci posset . . .
>
> . . . .
>
> Nec fructus idem arboribus constare solerent
> Sed mutarentur : ferre omnes omnia possent.[1]

But when the problem is limited, when it is only a
question of one species, of man, then Helvétius no
longer has such doubts. He declares positively and
with great confidence that all " differences " in people
lie in their development, and not in their embryos,
not in their heredity. At our birth we all share
similar qualities. Only education makes us dissimilar
from one another. We shall see again below that this

---

[1] Any species may develop from everything. . . . Trees do
not bear always the same fruit, but are variable : all things
may bring forth any species.

thought, though without solid foundation, is very fruitful in his hands. But he approaches it by a false path, and this origin of his thought can be felt every time he makes use of it and every time he tries to prove it. It shows that Diderot was perfectly right when he said that the statements of Helvétius are much stronger than his proofs. The metaphysical method of 18th century materialism constantly avenges itself upon the boldest and most logical of its followers.

We always seek physical pleasure and avoid physical suffering. An important statement. But how is it proved? Helvétius always takes a grown man with " passions ", the causes of which are extremely numerous and complicated and undoubtedly owe their origin to social environment, i.e. to the history of the species, and tries to deduce these " passions " from physical sensations. What arises independently of consciousness is represented to us as the immediate temporary fruit of this very consciousness. Habit and instinct assume the form of thought which inspires this feeling or that in man. In our essay on Holbach we explained that this mistake was characteristic of all the " philosophers " who defend a utilitarian morality. But in Helvétius this mistake assumes a scale which is really regrettable. In the picture drawn for us by Helvétius thought in the real sense of the word disappears, yielding place to a number of images which all belong without exception to " physical sensations ". This sensation which is, without doubt, the actual, and very remote cause of our moral habits, is transformed into the final cause of our acts. Thus the problem is solved by a fiction. But it is perfectly obvious that it is impossible to dissolve the problem in the acid of fiction. Further, by his " analysis " Helvétius deprives our moral feelings of their specific qualities and in this way erases that very x, the unknown quantity, the meaning of which he tries to define. He wishes to prove that all our feelings may be deduced from physical sensation. To prove this he invents a man who is always pursuing corporeal pleasures, " beautiful slaves ", etc. In fact this statement is stronger than its proof.

After our explanations there is no need for us to show, as La Harpe and many others have done, that Newton did not undertake his immense calculations in order to possess a beautiful mistress. Of course not ! But this truth does not bring us one step forward either in the science of " man " or in the history of philo- sophy. There are many more important things in science than the discovery of such " truths ".

Can it be seriously thought that Helvétius repre- sented man only in the form of a voluptuous, reasoning being?

It is sufficient merely to glance at his works to be convinced that this was not the case. Helvétius, for example, knew very well that there exist people who, " carried away by the spirit into the future and satisfied beforehand of the praise and regard of posterity ", sacrifice the glory and regard of the present for the distant hope of greater glory and regard,—people who in the main " seek the regard only of those citizens worthy of regard ".[1] Evidently these people foresee that they will not get much physical pleasure. Helvétius even expresses the opinion that there are persons for whom nothing higher than justice exists. And he declares that the ideal of justice is closely bound up with the ideal of happiness in the recollection of these persons. Both these ideas represent to such a degree a single whole that it is impossible to separate them from one another. People are accustomed to recall them simultaneously and " in so far as such a habit is established they always take pride in acting justly and virtuously. There exists nothing which they will not sacrifice for the sake of this lofty pride ".[2] Evidently these people, in order to be just, no longer need the stimulation of voluptuous images. Our philosopher expresses moreover, the opinion that education makes man just and unjust, that the power of education is unlimited, that " the moral man is the result of education and imitation ".[3] He expresses himself as follows upon the mechanism of our feelings and the force of the association of ideas. " If owing to the form of government I have everything to fear from the great, I shall mechanically respect greatness even in a foreign

[1] " De l'Homme ", Section IV, Chap. VI.
[2] Ibid., Chap. X, the last note to this Chapter.
[3] Ibid., Chap. XXII.

lord who has no power over me. If in my memory
I have associated the idea of virtue with that of happiness, I shall cultivate it even if this memory is the object
of persecution. I know well that in the long run these
two ideas will be separated, but it will be the work of
time, and of a very long time. . . . It is by profoundly
meditating upon this fact that we find the solution to
an infinite number of moral problems which could
never be solved other than by acquaintance with this
association of our ideas ".[1]

But what does all this mean? A cluster of contradictions of which one is more daring than the
other? Undoubtedly! The metaphysicians are often
the victims of such contradictions. To contradict themselves at every step is their professional disease, the only
means they have of reconciling their " either or ".
Helvétius is far from being an exception to this general
rule. On the contrary, having a lively and enterprising
mind he pays more often than the others in this coin
for the mistake of his methods. It is necessary to state
this mistake and in this way to show the advantages
of the dialectical method, but it should not be thought
that we may get rid of these mistakes by some misplaced
moral indignation and a few infinitely petty truths
which are already as old as the world.

" When you read him," La Harpe says about our
philosopher, " you notice that his imagination is
inspired only by brilliant and voluptuous thoughts and

[1] Ibid., Section VIII, Chap. IV.

that nothing in them corresponds to the spirit of philosophy ".[1] This should mean that Helvétius only spoke about " physical sensation " and made it the starting point of his investigations because he himself leaned much towards sensual pleasures. There are many stories about his love for " fair mistresses "; this love has been represented as being a supplement to his vanity. We will refrain from any judgement on such " critical " methods. But it is interesting to compare Helvétius and Chernyshevsky in this respect. The great Russian encyclopaedist was anything you please, but he was not " elegant ", nor a " farmer general ", nor " vain " (nobody ever accused him of such a weakness), nor a lover of " beautiful slaves ". But nevertheless, of all the French philosophers in the 18th century Helvétius most of all resembles him. Chernyshevsky was distinguished by the same fearless logic, by the same contempt for sentimentality, by the same method, by the same kind of taste, by the same rationalist method of argument, by the same inferences and examples, even to the most trifling, for the proof of this or that statement.[2] How is such a coincidence

[1] " Réfutation du livre de l'Esprit," p. 5.
[2] Helvétius recommends following the example of the geometricians. " If a complicated problem in mechanics is put before them, what do they do? They simplify it. They calculate the speed of bodies in motion without regard to their density, to the resistance of surrounding fluids, to the action of other bodies, etc." " De l'Homme ", Section IX, Chap. I. In almost the same terms Chernyshevsky recommends the

to be explained? Is it plagiarism on the part of the Russian writer? So far no one has dared to make such an accusation against Chernyshevsky. But let us go so far as to admit that the charge has some foundation. Then we should have to say that Chernyshevsky stole the ideas of Helvétius, who in his turn owed them to his voluptuous temperament and measureless vanity. This would certainly reveal astonishing clarity of mind and a deep philosophy of the history of human thought!

In noting the mistakes of Helvétius it should not be forgotten that he erred precisely at that point at which all idealist (or, it would be better to say, dualist)

simplification of the problems of political economy. Helvétius was accused of slandering Socrates and Regulus. But what Chernyshevsky says about the famous suicide of the chaste Lucrece who did not wish to survive her shame is astonishingly like the remarks of Helvétius upon the heroic prisoner of the Carthaginians. Chernyshevsky proposed that political economy should be chiefly concerned not with what is, but what should be. Compare this with what Helvétius says in his letter to Montesquieu: " Do you remember that in discussing your principles with you at Bréda I agreed that they are applicable to the present state of affairs, but that a writer who desires to be of use to men ought rather to concern himself with true maxims for a better future order of things, than to canonise those which become dangerous the moment that prejudice seizes on them in order to use and perpetuate them." (" Œuvres complètes d'Helvétius," Paris 1818, III, p. 261.) Many others might be added to this characteristic example. But we prefer to show the coincidence of views of these two writers, separated from one another by almost a century, only in so far as this assists our explanation of the theories of Helvétius.

philosophy erred in its struggle against French materialism. Spinoza and Leibnitz occasionally knew how to
make very good use of the dialectical weapon (the latter
particularly in his " Nouveaux essais sur l'entendement
humain ") but nevertheless their general outlook was
metaphysical. Moreover, Leibnitz and Spinoza were
far from playing a leading part in official French
philosophy in the 18th century. At this time a more
or less diluted variety of Cartesianism prevailed. But
the Cartesians did not have the slightest idea of
development.[1] A helplessness in method was to a
considerable extent the heritage assumed by materialism from its dualist predecessors. We should not,
however, be deceived in this respect. If the materialists were wrong, this still does not prove that their
opponents were right. Far from it: their opponents
were doubly and trebly mistaken, in a word, incom-
parably more mistaken.

What does La Harpe tell us about the origin of our
moral sentiments, La Harpe, who would surely never
let pass a chance of attacking Helvétius with the whole
of the good old philosophical artillery? Alas, very

---

[1] " Descartes ", says Flint, " shows incidentally in many
passages of his writings that he had looked on social facts with
a clear keen eye. And so does Malebranche." But the same
Flint recognises that " of a science of history Descartes had no
notion whatever. It was only with the decay of Cartesianism
that historical science began to flourish in France ". (" The
Philosophy of History in France and Germany ", Edinburgh
and London 1874, p. 76-78.)

little! He declares that " All our passions are given us directly by nature "; that they " *belong to our nature* (the emphasis is La Harpe's), although they are liable to excesses which are only possible thanks to the corruption of great societies "; that " society is in a natural condition " and " that therefore Helvétius was absolutely wrong to call artificial that which depends upon a natural and necessary order "; that man has " another measure of his judgement than his own interest ", and that " this measure is the sentiment of justice "; that " pleasure and suffering are the sole motives only of the lower animals ", but that " man should be guided by God, conscience and the laws, in accordance with his consciousness of them ".[1] Very profound indeed! Now at last everything is clear!

Let us now meet another opponent of our " sophist ". This time we have to do with a 19th century personage. Reading in " On the Spirit " that the measure of virtue is the general interest, that every society considers those acts virtuous which are useful to us, and that the judgements of people upon actions and their fellows change in accordance with their interests, he triumphantly hurls at us the following harangue: " If it is declared that popular judgements upon various actions have the right of infallibility in so far as they have behind them the majority of individuals, then a number of conclusions may be drawn from this principle, each one more stupid than the last, as for

[1] " Réfutation du livre de l'Esprit ", p. 57, 61, 63, 68, 69.

example: only majority opinion is true . . . truth becomes error when it ceases to be the opinion of the majority and is transformed into the opinion of the minority, and vice versa . . . error becomes truth when it becomes the opinion of the majority after it has been for a long time the opinion of the minority ".[1] A naïve person! His refutation of Helvétius, whose theories he has not even succeeded in understanding, is certainly " novel ".

Even more important critics, such as Lange, for example, have seen in this teaching merely the apologia of " personal interest ". It is considered an axiom that Adam Smith's moral teaching has nothing in common with the ethics of the French materialist. These two teachings are mutual antitheses. Lange, who rates Helvétius very low, speaks with great respect of Adam

---

[1] " Nouvelle réfutation du livre de l'Esprit ", à Clermont-Ferrand, 1817, p. 46. The method of argument of the anonymous author recalls the argumentation of the very learned— " learned! "—Damiron. At the commencement of " On the Spirit " Helvétius says that man owes his intellectual superiority over animals among other things to the construction of his extremities. " You think," thunders Damiron, " that horses if they were given a man's hands would also be given his reason? Nothing like it would take place, the horse would merely prove incapable of living as a horse ". (" Mémoires pour servir à l'histoire de la philosophie au XVIII Siècle ", Paris 1858, I, p. 406.) A certain naïve professor of divinity in St. Petersburg disputed Darwin's theory in the same way: " Darwin says: ' Throw a fowl into the water and it will grow webbed feet '. I declare that the fowl will simply drown ".

Smith as a moralist. " Adam Smith's discovery of morality in sympathy ", he says, " although even at that time it was not argued with sufficient consistency, is nevertheless even up to our own day one of the most fruitful attempts to find a natural and rational basis for morality ". The French commentator on the " Theory of Moral Sentiments ", G. Bodrillard, considers Smith's teaching a healthy reaction " against the system of materialism and egoism ". Smith himself felt very little " sympathy " towards the materialist teaching on morality. The theory of Helvétius, like the theory of Mandeville, must have seemed " licentious " to him. And in fact Smith's theory seems at first glance the direct opposite of what we find in the works of Helvétius. The reader, we hope, has not forgotten how the latter explained regret at the loss of a friend. Let us now read what the famous Englishman has written : " We sympathise even with the dead . . . It is miserable, we think, to be deprived of the light of the sun; to be shut out from life and conversation; to be laid in the cold grave, a prey to corruption and the reptiles of the earth; to be no more thought of in this world, but to be obliterated in a little time, from the affections, and almost from the memory, of their dearest friends and relations . . . That our sympathy can afford them no consolation seems to be an addition to their calamity." . . . etc.[1] This, of course, is

[1] " The Theory of Moral Sentiments ", London 1873, 12-13. This work first appeared in 1757.

something quite different! But let us examine this argument a little more closely. What does Adam Smith's "sympathy" mean? "However selfish so-ever man may be supposed, there are evidently some principles in his nature, which interest him in the fortune of others, and render their happiness necessary to him, though he derives nothing from it, except the pleasure of seeing it . . . that we often derive sorrow from the sorrow of others, is a matter of fact too obvious to require any instances to prove it". The source of such sensibility to the sufferings of others is to be found in the fact that " as we have no immediate experience of what other men feel, we can form no idea of the manner in which they are affected, but by conceiving what we ourselves should feel in a like situation ".[1] Perhaps you think that there is nothing in the works of Helvétius resembling this theory of sympathy? In his book " On Man " (Section II, Chap. VII) the latter asks " What is a humane man? " and answers " He for whom the sight of another's misfortune is a painful sight ". But whence comes this capacity for feeling for the suffering of another? We owe it to memory which teaches us to identify ourselves with others. " If a child has contracted the habit of identifying itself with the unfortunate he will, once he has got this habit, be the more affected by their unhappiness because, in deploring their lot, he will be touched by the condition of humanity in general and

[1] Ibid., p. 9-10.

his own in particular.   An infinite variety of feelings
will then mingle with this first feeling and from their
assemblage there will be formed this total sentiment of
pleasure felt by a noble soul in helping the unfortunate,
a sentiment he is not always capable of analysing."

It must be recognised that Smith regards the starting
point of his argument, sympathy, in the same way as
Helvétius.   True, Helvétius connects sympathy with
other, less " sympathetic " feelings.   In his opinion,
" we help the unfortunate: 1. To avoid the physical
pain of seeing them suffer.   2. To enjoy the sight of a
gratitude which at least inspires us with a confused
hope of deriving some distant benefit.   3. To perform
an act of power, the exercise of which is always pleasant
to us, because it always recalls to our mind the image
of the pleasures bound up with this power.   4. Because
in a good education the idea of happiness is always
associated with the idea of benevolence, and this benevolence, by bringing us the esteem and affection of men,
may, like wealth, be regarded as a power or a means
of avoiding suffering and securing pleasure ".   Of
course this is already different from Smith's view,
though as regards sympathy their views are similar.
But it shows how Helvétius arrives at results absolutely
the opposite of the conclusions of the author of " The
Theory of Moral Sentiments ".   For the latter the
sentiment of sympathy is founded in our " nature ",
for Helvétius there is only " physical sensation " in our
nature.   He sees himself compelled to analyse what

Smith did not even think of touching upon. Smith moves forward in one direction. Helvétius chooses the directly opposite one. What is there astonishing if they fall further and further apart so that finally they meet no longer?

Helvétius was undoubtedly not at all inclined to let all our sentiments pass through the stage of sympathy as one of the steps in their development. In this respect he is not " onesided ". But neither should it be thought that Smith's " sympathy " forced him to renounce completely a utilitarian outlook. For him, as for Helvétius, the public interest is the foundation and sanction of morality.[1] But it never occurs to him to deduce these foundations and sanctions from the primal elements of human nature. He never asks the question, what is the foundation of that " higher wisdom " which guides human inclinations. He sees a bare fact where Helvétius already sees a process of development. Smith says that " the understanding of human nature which derives all our passions and senti-

---

[1] " We do not love our country merely as a part of the great society of mankind—we love it for its own sake, and independently of any such consideration. That wisdom which contrived the system of human affections, as well as that of every other part of nature, seems to have judged that the interest of the great society of mankind would be best promoted by directing the principle of each individual to that particular portion of it which was most within the sphere both of his abilities and of his understanding " (p. 203 and 204 of the above English edition).

116

ments from self-love . . . evidently arose from a confused and incorrect idea of the system of sympathy ".[1]
He might have said that this system tries to discover the origin of our passions and sentiments whilst he himself was satisfied with a more or less adequate description of them.[2]

The contradictions in which Helvétius is entangled are, as we have already more than once remarked, the consequences of his metaphysical method. In addition, many of the contradictions encountered in his work are caused by the fact that he often limited his theoretical point of view in order that he might more easily emphasise definite practical aims. A good instance of this is his " slandering " of Regulus.

He shows that as a warrior and granted the morals of the ancient Romans, Regulus could not have acted otherwise than he did, even if he were only pursuing his own personal interest. This is the " slander "

[1] Ibid., p. 281.
[2] This is very simple and evidently difficult to understand. " Virtue is undoubtedly beneficial," says Huxley, " but the man is to be envied to whom her ways seem in any wise playful . . . the calculation of the greatest happiness is not performed quite so easily as a rule of three sum . . . in whichever way we look at the matter, morality is based on feeling, not on reason." (" Hume ", p. 205-207.) If the famous English scientist thinks he can refute the materialist morality of the 18th century by such arguments he is very much mistaken and forgets his teacher Darwin. However, he evidently has in view only epigones like Bentham and J. S. Mill. In this case he is right.

against which Jean-Jacques objected. But Helvétius is far from conveying that Regulus was actually following only his own interest. "The behaviour of Regulus, was, without doubt, the consequence of the fiery enthusiasm which led him to virtue". But in this case what does he mean by his "slander"? He wishes to show that "such enthusiasm could only arise in Rome". Owing to the "perfection" of the republican system of government the personal interests of its citizens were bound up as closely as possible with the interests of the state.[1] Hence the heroism of the ancient Romans. The practical conclusion: it is only necessary to know how to act to-day in the same way and we shall see that people just as heroic as Regulus will arise. Helvétius shows only one side of the medal, wishing to fix the attention of his readers upon it. But this does not prove that he had overlooked the effects of habit, of the association of ideas, of "sympathy", "enthusiasm", of noble pride, etc. etc. Far from it. He merely did not always know how to trace the connection between these effects and personal interest and "physical sensation", although he tried at the same time to expose it, since he never forgot that man is only sensation. If he does not succeed in this task, then the cause is to be found in the metaphysical character of materialism in his epoch. He can, however, always claim that he deduced all the consequences arising from his main premise.

[1] "De l'Esprit", discours III, Chap XXII.

The same prevalence of practical aims explains his trivial attitude towards the question of whether all people are born with the same abilities. He did not even succeed in posing this question correctly. But what did he mean in this matter? Grimm understood this very well, although he was far from being a master in the sphere of theory. In his " Correspondence " (November 1773) he speaks of the book " On Man ": " Its chief aim is to show that the geniuses, virtues, talents, to which the nations owe their greatness and happiness are not the result either of different nourishment, or of different temperaments, or of the organs of the five senses, upon which law and government have no influence, but they are the result of education, in regard to which laws and government are all-powerful ".[1] It is easy to understand what practical

---

[1] Holbach did not share the opinion of Helvétius, whom, by the way, he calls " the famous moralist ". In his opinion, " it is a mistake to think that education can do everything with a man; it can only make use of the material provided by nature; it can only sow successfully in the soil provided by nature ". (Cf. " La Morale Universelle," Section V, Chap. III; Cf. the same work Section I, Chap. IV.) Holbach does not ask what part society plays in the formation of that which he calls the nature of an individual. Helvétius himself, by the way, knew that his view could not be proved, strictly speaking. He merely thought that at least it might be stated, " that this influence (i.e. the influence of social organisation on the mind of the average normal individual) is so insignificant that it may be looked on as the negligible quantity which is disregarded in algebraical calculations, and that what has hitherto

value such a view can have in a period of revolutionary ferment.

If man is only a machine and if this machine, set in motion by " physical sensation ", is forced to do everything which this sensation demands, then the role of " free will " is of no account in either the history of a nation or the life of an individual. If " physical sensation " is the principle of the will, needs, passions, society, thoughts, judgement and acts of people, then the key to the historical fate of the human race must not be sought either in people or in their " nature "; if all people have similar spiritual qualities, then the supposed peculiarities of race and national character can clearly explain nothing in either the contemporary or the previous conditions of this or that nation. These three logical and inevitable conclusions already comprise very important prolegomena to the whole philosophy of history. According to Helvétius, all nations which are in a similar position, have similar laws, a similar spirit, similar passions. In consequence of this, " we find the morals of the ancient Germans among the Indians "; in consequence of this, " Asia, largely inhabited by Malayans, is ruled by our ancient feudal laws "; in consequence of this " fetishism was not only

been attributed to the influence of physical properties and which could not be explained by this cause, is fully explained by moral causes " (i.e. the influence of social environment— G.P.). Chernyshevsky speaks in almost the same terms of the influence of race on the historical fate of nations.

the origin of religion but its cult, still preserved throughout almost the whole of Africa even in our time, was once general throughout the world." In consequence of this same cause, Greek mythology has many features similar to the mythology of the Celts. Through the same cause, finally, the same proverbs are often found among very different nations. There exists in general an astonishing analogy in the institutions, spirit and faith of primitive nations. Nations, like individuals, are much more like one another than often appears to be the case.

Interest, needs, these are the most important and the only teachers of the human race. Why is hunger a common cause of human actions? Because of all needs it is the one most often repeated, the most insistent, the one which makes itself the most felt. Hunger sharpens the minds of animals; it compels us, human beings, to the exercise of our abilities, although we imagine that we are greatly superior to the animal. It teaches the savage to bend the bow, to weave a net, to place traps for his victims. " In the same way in all civilised nations hunger brings all citizens into activity, teaching them to cultivate the earth, teaching them crafts and the fulfilment of different duties ". Humanity owes to it the art of making the earth fruitful with the plough, in the same way as it owes the art of building and making clothes to the necessity of defence against the severity of the weather. Without needs man would have no stimulus to action. " One of the chief causes of the ignorance and laziness of the Africans is the fruitfulness of that part of the globe which they inhabit; they can satisfy all their needs almost without any cultivation. The African has no interest in thinking. Therefore he thinks very little. The same can be said of the Caribbean. If he is less industrious than the savages of North America then the cause is to be found in the fact that the latter are in greater need of industry ". Need is the exact measure of the exercise of the intensity of the human spirit. " In some respects the inhabitants of Kamchatka are distinguished by unexampled stupidity : in others they are distinguished by astonishing agility. In the ability to prepare clothing . . . they surpass Europeans. Why? Because they live in parts of the earth remarkable for a particular severity of climate and in which the need for clothing generally makes itself felt before everything else. And a common need is always the most effective ".[1]

But if we " owe the art of cultivating the earth " to need, then this art, once it is discovered and practised, begins to have a great and decisive influence on our institutions, our thoughts and sentiments. " The

[1] This brings us to the question of the influence of climate. But the reader will see that here it is not the immediate influence of climate on the morality of people which is spoken of, and to which Montesquieu referred. In the opinion of Helvétius this influence is felt through the intermediary of the arts, i.e. thanks to a more or less rapid development of productive forces. These are two completely different points of view.

inhabitant of the forest, a naked man, who knows no speech, can, of course, form a clear and accurate idea of strength or weakness, but not of justice and legality ". These ideas presuppose society; they change together with the interests of society. Why was theft permitted in Sparta? Why did they punish thieves caught in the act only for their clumsiness? What can be stranger than such a custom? " If we remember, however, the laws of Lycurgus and the contempt felt in the republic towards gold and silver, when the laws recognised only heavy and unwieldy iron money, then it becomes understandable that the only possible kind of theft was that of fowls and vegetables. Always carried out with agility and often obstinately resisted, such thefts taught the Lacedae-monian manliness and vigilance. The law permitting robbery might be useful to this nation ". . . . The Skythians had a different attitude. They considered theft to be the greatest crime. Their manner of life made such a view inevitable for them. " Their scattered herds wandered over the valleys. How easy to steal them ! And what disorder would result if such thefts were tolerated. Therefore, to use Aristotle's expression, with them the law was made the protector of the herds ". Nations whose whole wealth was in herds had no need of private property in land; this first appears among the tillers of the soil for whom it is almost an absolute necessity. Savage nations, wandering through the forests, know only temporary and accidental unions between man and woman. Settled and agricultural nations introduce indissoluble marriage. "Whilst the husband makes the earth fruitful with his plough, the wife feeds the poultry, waters the cattle, shears the sheep, looks after the household and the yard, prepares food for her husband, for the children and the servants." Hence the indissolubility of marriage, far from being here a heavy yoke for the husband and wife, is on the contrary of the greatest benefit to them. The laws which regulate marriage in Catholic countries are founded on these relations. They are therefore suited only to the interests and professions of agricultural workers. On the other hand they are a great hindrance to the people of other professions, particularly to the "strong", the "rich" and the "idle", who see in love not a means of satisfying real and often very insistent needs, but a distraction, a remedy against boredom. The picture of the family morals of the parasitic classes in society drawn by Count Leo Tolstoi in his "Kreutzer Sonata" and before him by Fourier, in its chief features recalls what Helvétius said about marriage and love among "the idle".

The character of a nation occupied in agriculture is necessarily different from the character of a nomad nation. "In every country there is a definite quantity of objects which education presents to all alike, and the similar impression from these objects engenders in citizens that agreement in thoughts and sentiments which is called the national spirit and the national character."

But it is not hard to understand that these " objects," the influence of which has such a decisive importance for education, are not the same for nations living in such different conditions as, for example, agriculture and hunting. It is just as obvious that national character changes. The French are considered a cheerful people. But they were not always so. The Emperor Julian said of the Parisians: " I like them because their character, like mine, is strictly serious ".[1] But look at the Romans. What strength, virtue, love of freedom, what hatred of slavery in the epoch of the Republic! And what weakness, cowardice and baseness since the rise of the Cæsars! Even Tiberius found this baseness unbearable. Moreover, a nation's

---

[1] As for the contemporary Frenchmen, Helvétius remarks that the French nation cannot be happy for " unfortunate times have forced its rulers to impose heavy taxes on the country, so that the agricultural class, which is two-thirds of the nation, lives in poverty and poverty is never cheerful ". He laughs at the usual style of describing national character. " In general there is nothing more comical and untrue than the pictures describing the character of different nations. Some describe their nation after the image of contemporary society and, in accordance with this, represent it as pitiful, happy, crude, intelligent. Others copy what thousands of writers have written before them: they never try to investigate the changes which the changes in government and morals inevitably create in the character of a nation ". (" De l'Esprit ", discours III, Chap. XXX.)

character does not only change with historical events; at any given moment it is not the same even in different professions. The tastes and habits of the military class are not the same as the tastes and habits of the priests, the tastes and habits of " the idle " are not the same as the tastes and habits of the tillers of the soil and the artisans. All these differences depend on education. Education makes of a woman a being subordinated to a man. But this subordination is not the same among all the estates of society. Sovereigns (" women " like Elizabeth, Catherine II, etc.[1]) are in no way behind men in genius. The same applies to ladies of the Court. " They are distinguished by the same intelligence as their husbands ". The reason of this is that despite all differences in position both sexes in this class " get any equally bad education ".

Different ideas of beauty are formed thanks to the impressions of childhood. " If the image of some definite woman particularly delights me it will be imprinted in my memory as an image of beauty, and I shall judge other women by their more or less close resemblance to this image. Hence the difference in tastes ". So this is a matter of habit. But since the habits of any nation are not always the same, then its

[1] Catherine II managed to deceive Helvétius as she did many others. He always refers to her with great admiration. He was convinced that the Northern Messalina attacked Poland in the interests of toleration.

tastes and opinions on the beauty of different objects in nature and art will also change.[1] " Why do mediaeval novels not please us? Why did the style of Corneille please more during the lifetime of the famous poet than it does at present? (Of course, he refers to the epoch of Helvétius.—G.P.) Because this was the time of the League and the Fronde, a time of disorders, when minds which were still inflamed by the fire of revolt were able to judge more boldly and better upon courageous feelings, and were more receptive to ambition; because the character which Corneille gives to his heroes, the plans which occupied their ambition, were closer to the spirit of his time than to that of our own when very few heroes and ambitious persons are encountered and when after many storms a happy calm has supervened and the volcano of revolt is everywhere extinguished ".

In order the better to understand the views of Helvétius upon the role of " interest " in human history we will dwell a little more upon the Robinsonade which he invented. His Robinsonade is " a few families who have gone away onto an island ". Their first care is to build huts and cultivate the soil necessary for their existence. If their island has more land

[1] What Helvétius has to say about our judgement on beauty to a certain extent contains the germs of Chernyshevsky's aesthetic theory. But only the germs. The analysis of the Russian author goes much farther into this sphere and leads to much more important results.

suitable for cultivation than these first colonists need then they will almost all be equally rich; the wealthier among them will be those who have stronger arms and greater energy. Their interests are therefore not very complicated and " so it will be sufficient for them to have a few laws ". If they see themselves compelled to elect a leader then this leader will still remain an agriculturist like the other members of the colony. "The only advantage which might be given him is that of choosing his plot of ground for himself. In all other respects he will enjoy no power ".

But gradually the population of our island will increase; it will become very crowded; the reserve of free land which might be occupied will be exhausted. What must then be done with those who have no landed property? Leaving out of consideration robbery, theft, or emigration, they have to find some refuge for themselves in new inventions. Those of them who succeed in inventing some new article of consumption or luxury which has any kind of wide distribution, will live by the exchange of their products for the products of the agriculturists and other artisans. It may be that such a one will become the founder of a manufactory which he will "equip in a pleasant and convenient place, usually on the banks of a river, the branches of which flow deep into the country, thanks to which the transport of his goods is made easy ". Of course he will not remain the only industrialist on the island. The continued multiplication of the inhabitants will lead to the invention of other articles of luxury or of consumption and new manufactories will spring up. A few such manufactories will first form a village and then an important town. "This town will soon be inhabited by the richest citizens since the profits of trade are always enormous when a small number of merchants have only a few competitors." The rich agriculturists will leave their estates in order to dwell in the town for at least a few months in each year. The poor will follow them in the hope of more easily finding a living. In a word, our town will be transformed into a capital.

Thus we have rich and poor, entrepreneurs and simple workers. Primitive equality has disappeared. Now our nation under one and the same name unites "an infinite quantity of different nations, whose interests are more or less opposed." There will be as many nations as there are classes. And this process of the formation of classes with different and even opposed interests is inevitable in the history of nations. It takes place more or less quickly, but nevertheless takes place and always will take place. "It is necessary that the more industrious should earn more, that the economic should save more and obtain fresh riches to add to those already won. In addition there are heirs in receipt of great inheritances. Merchants exist who load great quantities of goods upon their ships and in this way earn great means because every commerce adds money to money. The unequal distribution of money is therefore the necessary effect of its introduction into the state ".

But this necessary effect brings with it no less necessary consequences. Those who have nothing, and their number gradually increases thanks to the multiplication of citizens, begin to compete more and more among themselves in order to find some occupation. They cut down ever further their level of life. The consequence of this inequality becomes ever greater; poverty is ever more widespread; " the poor man sells and the rich buys ", and the number of property owners becomes very small. Then the laws become ever more strict. Mild laws are suited to ruling a nation of property owners. " With the Germans, the Gauls and the Scandinavians the laws which punish different misdemeanours only fixed more or less high fines ". This changed when the property-less became the great majority of the nation. He who has nothing cannot answer with his substance and has to be punished in person : hence corporal punishments. The greater the number of the poor, the more thefts, robberies and crimes there will be. It is necessary to have recourse to violence in order to contend against them. The man who has no property easily changes his dwelling place. So the guilty can easily escape punishment. It therefore becomes necessary to arrest citizens with the observation of as little formality as possible, often at the first suspicion. " But arrest is already a punishment with the help of violence, which quickly begins to be applied even to property owners and replaces freedom by slavery ". Corporal punishments in their turn are at first applied only to the poor, and are then also passed on to the property owners. " All citizens alike are subordinated to the bloody laws. Everything unites to bring them to life ".

The increase in the number of citizens leads to the rise of representative government, since it is no longer possible for all citizens to meet in one place to discuss public affairs. So long as citizens are almost equal among themselves their representatives adopt laws in accordance with public opinion. But as primitive equality disappears, as the interests of citizens grow more complex, the representatives begin to separate their interests from the interests of those they represent; they become independent of their constituents, they gradually acquire power equal to the power of the whole nation. " Surely it is clear that the separation of the interests of the governed in a great inhabited country must always give the rulers the means of acquiring authority which man's natural love for power will ever make the object of their desires. Certainly on the one hand, property owners exclusively occupied with their property " cease to be citizens "; on the other hand, people without property are for them enemies whom a tyrant or tyrants can arm against the property owners at their discretion. Thus " mental laziness " in the constituents and an active desire for power in the representatives produce an immense change in the state. Everything favours " ambition " at the right moment. Freedom dies, the prospects of despotism become ever greater. So the multiplication of citizens leads to the rise of representative government. The contradiction of their interests leads to the domination of tyranny.

In one part of his book " On Man ", to which we have chiefly referred in the foregoing explanation, Helvétius says that in his conclusions he follows " experience and Xenophon ". These are very characteristic words. Like Holbach and the other " philosophers " of his time he saw the role of class struggle in history fairly clearly. But he went further than " Xenophon ", i.e. the authors of antiquity, in his estimation of the latter. In his opinion the class struggle always engendered tyranny and nothing but tyranny. For him people " without property " are simply a dangerous weapon in the hands of ambitious rich men. They can do nothing but strive to sell themselves to anyone " who wants to buy them ". Here he has in mind, not the modern proletariat, but the ancient, and particularly the Roman. In accordance with this the social movement is for him only a vicious circle. " Let us suppose that some person or other has grown rich through commerce and joined to his substance a large number of small persons. From this the number of property owners has grown less and with it the number of those whose interests are more closely connected with the national interests, but at the same time the number of people without property and with no interests in public affairs has grown. But if such people are continually in the service of those who pay them, then how can one imagine that the powerful will never make use of them for the subordination of his fellow citizens to his own will? This is the necessary consequence of the too great multiplication of persons in the state. This is the circle which hitherto all have recognised but which a very large number of different governments have completed ".

Helvétius was a long way from feeling the same mistrust of the English as Holbach. He finds, moreover, that the social and political conditions in Great Britain leave much to be desired, but he respected the country as the most enlightened and free in the world. Yet he considered that this English freedom, with which he so sympathised, was not very stable. He considered that the difference in interests which in England went so far, sooner or later must lead to its inevitable consequence, to the appearance of despotism. It must be admitted that the history of Ireland at least does not altogether prove him mistaken.

Our philosopher's views on the question of the multiplication of people once more show how little there was original in the teaching of Malthus. We will not criticise these views here, any more than his views on the history of primitive property and the family. It was enough for us to note the general historical and philosophical outlook of Helvétius.[1]   But to complete our summary, we should first examine a few other consequences of " the multiplication of citizens " or, to express it more correctly, the continual and inevitable growth of inequality of condition.

There is nothing more dangerous for society than the existence of people without property.   There is nothing more profitable to the entrepeneurs than such people, for nobody can better serve their interests. " The greater the number of poor, the less the entrepeneurs will pay for their labour ".   But in " a commercial country " the entrepeneurs are now the real power.   The public interest is sacrificed to the advantage of their " private interest ", which is the motive of their actions and the criterion of their judgements. We see this in any society with complicated and opposed interests.   It disintegrates into small societies which judge the virtue, intelligence and merits of citizens from the point of view of their own interests. Finally the interest of the powerful has the greatest command over the nation and their voice receives the greatest attention.

We already know that corruption of morals appears everywhere where private interest is separated from

[1] Let us remark by the way that Holbach approached the " multiplication of citizens " from exactly the opposite point of view.   For him it only meant the increase of the strength and wealth of the State.   In this he was in agreement with the majority of writers in the 18th century.

public. Evergrowing inequality in conditions must therefore engender and increase the corruption of morals. This is what happens in practice. Money, which helps the progress of inequality, at the same time brings about the degeneration of virtue. In a country " where money is not in circulation ", the nation is the only just distributor of reward. " General respect and the gift of public gratitude may there be rendered only to ideas and acts which are beneficial to the nation and therefore every citizen is there compelled to virtue ". In countries where money is in circulation its owner can give it to this person or that who gives him the greater amount of pleasure, and generally he does act in this way. As a consequence of this, rewards are often given for actions which are " useful only for the rich, but harmful for society ". Rewards given to vice engender vicious persons and the love of money, stifling every spirit, every patriotic virtue, creates only base characters, frauds and intriguers. " It is impossible to extend love of wealth among all classes of citizens without inspiring the ruling group with a desire for robbery and abuses. Then they begin to equip harbours, to take up arms, to start up trading companies, to go to war, which is undertaken, as they like to say, for the honour of the nation; in a word they pursue every pretext for robbery. Then simultaneously there begin to appear in the state all the vices engendered of greed, which in turn poison all its members and finally overthrow it ".

Holbach, as we have already shown in the essay we have devoted to him, considered love of wealth to be the mother of all vices, and fatal for a nation. But in Holbach we only meet declamation, whereas Helvétius tries to see through the laws of social development. Holbach thundered against " luxury ". Helvétius observes that luxury is merely the consequence of unequal distribution of wealth. Holbach demanded from the legislature a struggle against the desire for luxury; Helvétius considered such a struggle not merely useless, but even harmful for society. In the first place, laws against luxury, which are always easy to avoid, are too sharp an attack upon the right of property, " the most sacred of all rights ". Secondly, in order to destroy luxury, it is necessary to drive out money, " but not one sovereign can give way to such a plan, and even if it were proposed, no nation would be found to carry it out ". The realisation of such a plan would be absolutely fatal to the nation.

Luxury only exists where conditions are very unequal. In a state where approximate equality of conditions exists among the citizens luxury cannot exist, whatever stage of prosperity has been attained, or, more correctly, in such a state luxury will not be a misfortune but a great public benefit. But in so far as wealth is distributed extremely unevenly, the driving out of luxury will mean the cessation of the production of many articles and consequently the unemployment of a large number of poor persons. So the final result will be directly the opposite of what it was wished to achieve. " The discontent shown by the majority of moralists against luxury is the result of ignorance ", Helvétius concludes.[1]

So we have a constant law of social development. From poverty a nation arrives at wealth, from wealth at unequal distribution of wealth, at corruption of morals, at luxury, at vice; hence it proceeds to despotism, to its doom. " The law of life, which as it develops in a mighty oak tree and raises aloft its shoots, puts forth its branches, thickens its trunk and makes it the lord of the forest, is at the same time the law of the tree's doom ". And " under the existing form of government " nations cannot get away from this very dangerous path of development. It is even dangerous for them to slow down their steps along this road. Stagnation will mean incalculable catastrophe, may mean the cessation of life.

The quantity and particularly the character of the manufactures of any country depend on the wealth of the country and the method of their distribution. If all citizens are well-to-do, then they all wish to be well-dressed and so there arise many manufactures

[1] Thus he expresses himself in " On Man ". In " On the Spirit " Helvétius gives his opinion in an unclear form, but there also he allows it to be understood that the question of luxury cannot be solved so easily as the " moralists " suppose Diderot said that the place dealing with luxury belongs to the best in the book. Cf. his works, Vol. I, Chap. I, Article on " The Book ' On the Spirit ' ".

which work up cloth neither too fine nor too coarse. If, on the other hand, the majority of citizens are poor, then only those enterprises will exist which care for the needs of the wealthy class and they will only produce rich, brilliant and not very sound materials. So, " whatever the government, all phenomena depend upon one another ".

One of the most important sections of modern industry is the production of cotton goods. These goods are meant for the wealthy consumers. In this respect, the view of Helvétius does not coincide with reality.[1] But it nevertheless remains true that under any government all phenomena depend upon one another. We have already seen many examples of this and we will quote only one more.

Their need teaches people how to cultivate the soil, their need causes the birth of arts and science. Need also leads to their stagnation or to their forward movement in this direction or that. But in so far as we get a considerable inequality of conditions we see the rise of a number of arts for pleasure, the aim of which is to distract the wealthy and to relieve them of their boredom. Interest never ceases to be the only great

[1] Helvétius knows societies in which " money circulates " and others in which it does not. But in both the one and the other, products always assume for him the form of commodities. This seems as natural to him as private property. In general his economic views leave much to be desired. Even the best founded and most mature of them are no higher than the economic views of David Hume.

teacher of the human race. How can it be otherwise?
We should not forget that " any comparison of objects
between themselves presupposes attention, any attention
presupposes effort, and any effort a motive for its
application ". Indisputably the interests of every society
call for the support of education. But since the rewards
which are given to people for their services are not
always the portion of those who serve the general
interest, but very often of those who serve the interests
of powerful persons, then it is not hard to understand
why sciences, the arts and literature assume a direction
which coincides with the interests of these latter.
" Why should not the arts and sciences shine with the
greatest brilliance in a country like Greece, where they
enjoyed general and constant respect? " Why did Italy
have such an abundance of orators? Did she owe this
to the influence of climate as the learned imbecility
of certain academic pedants declared? An irrefutable
answer is to be found in the fact that Rome simultaneously lost both its rhetoric and its freedom. " Try
to explain on what were founded the reproaches of
barbarity and stupidity which the Greeks, Romans and
all Europeans have always made against the peoples of
the East, and you will find that the Eastern nations
were considered barbarians and fools by all the educated
nations of Europe, an object for the contempt of free
nations and of posterity because by the word ' mind '
these Eastern nations merely understood separate and
unconnected ideas which were useful to them, and

because throughout almost the whole of Asia despotism forbad the study of morality, metaphysics, jurisprudence and politics, in a word, almost all the sciences which interest humanity ". If, as was stated above, all nations which are in the same condition have the same laws, the same spirit, and the same inclinations, then this must be attributed to the influence of the same interests. The combination of interests determines the course of development of the human spirit.

The interest of the state, as of private persons, and as of all human affairs, experiences thousands of transformations. The same laws, habits and actions may be both useful and harmful to one and the same nation. It follows from this that one and the same laws may be now accepted, now rejected, that the same action may be called now virtuous, now vicious,—" a statement which it is impossible to refute without recognising that there may be actions which are simultaneously useful and harmful for the state, without thus undermining the basis of all legislation and of every society ".

The custom of killing the aged exists among many savage peoples. It appears at first as though there can be nothing more disgusting than this custom. But it is only necessary to think a little in order to recognise that these nations are compelled in their situation to consider the murder of the aged a virtuous act, that love for their old and decrepit relatives must compel the young people to act in this way. Savages do not have enough to live upon.   The aged are not in a condition to support themselves by hunting, since this calls for great physical strength.   They have therefore either to die by a lingering and wretched death or else to be a burden upon their children or upon the whole of society, which owing to its poverty is unable to bear such a burden.   It is therefore better to cut short these sufferings by the swift and necessary murder of parents. " This is the cause of this disgusting custom; for this reason a nomad people which is kept by its hunting and lack of means of existence for six months in a year in impassable forests, sees itself, as it were, forced to this barbarity; in this way parent-murder in these countries arises out of and is carried out on, the basis of the same principle of humanity which causes us to shudder at the perpetrators ".

Holbach asks why the positive laws of nations are so often in contradiction with the laws " of nature " and " of justice ".   He has a simple answer ready. " Evil laws," he says, " are the consequence either of the corruption of morals, or of the mistakes of society, or of tyranny which compels nature to bend before its authority ".[1] Such an answer does not satisfy Helvétius. He looks for " a real or, at least, an apparent benefit " in the shape of a cause for the laws and customs which are so lightly attributed to " corruption " or " errors ". " However stupid the nations may be considered," he says, " they have of course, being enlightened by their

[1] " Politique naturelle ", London 1773, I, p. 738.

own interests, not unreasonably assimilated the strange customs which exist among some of them; the fantastic character of these customs is therefore dependent upon the difference of interests of the nations ". Only those customs and laws are really deserving of hatred which still continue to exist after the causes of their introduction have disappeared and they have become harmful to society. " All customs bring only a transient advantage, like the scaffolding which is doomed to be demolished after a palace has been built ".

Such is the theory, and it leaves very little place for natural law, for absolute justice, if it leaves any place at all. At first it appeared dangerous even to such people as Diderot, who called it paradoxical. " In practice, public and private interest changes the ideas of justice and injustice; but the essence of these ideas is not dependent upon it ". But what is the essence of these ideas? And upon what does it depend? Diderot says nothing in regard to this. He quotes a few examples to prove that justice is absolute. But the examples are very empty ones. Is it not always and everywhere a praiseworthy act to give water to a man dying from thirst? Of course. But at the most this shows that there always exist interests which are common to humanity everywhere, for all time, during all phases of its development. " To give water to drink " takes us no further than the following argument of Voltaire: " If I demand back from a Turk, a Persian, or a native of Malabar money which I have

lent, then he will recognise that it is just to pay it "
. . . undoubtedly.   But how wretched this absolute
morality is, even though it is always considered as holy !
Locke says : " The people who declare that there exist
innate practical principles do not tell us what these
principles are ".   Helvétius might say the same concerning the supporters of " morality in general ".

It is perfectly clear that Helvétius' views on the
question of morality coincided absolutely with the
principles of materialist sensualism.   On the whole he
only repeated and developed the ideas of his teacher
Locke, who was at the same time also the teacher of
Holbach, Diderot and Voltaire.

" Good and evil for the English philosopher mean
only satisfaction or suffering.   Therefore in the moral
respect good and bad are what coincide or depart from
the law by means of which good and bad are brought
to us by the will and power of the legislature."   Long
before Helvétius Locke said : " Virtue is generally
approved, not because innate, but because profitable. . . .
He that will carefully peruse the history of mankind,
and look abroad into the several tribes of men, and with
indifference survey their actions, will be able to satisfy
himself that there is scarce that principle of morality
to be named, or rule of virtue to be thought on (those
only excepted that are absolutely necessary to hold
society together, which commonly too are neglected
betwixt distinct societies) which is not somewhere or
other slighted and condemned by the general fashion

of whole societies of men governed by practical opinions and rules of living quite opposite to others."

This is precisely what Helvétius tells us, but with this difference only, that Helvétius knows where to dot the i. Starting from " satisfaction " and " suffering ", he set himself the task of explaining by interest historical changes in the will of the legislator. This was perfectly logical, even too logical for the French " philosophers " in the 18th century. In fact the party of the philosophers was a fighting party. In its struggle against the system then existing it felt the need of basing itself on an authority less disputable than the authority of the constantly changing interests of people. They saw such an authority in " nature ". Morality and politics based on this foundation were nevertheless utilitarian: *Salus populi* (the good of the people) was still for them the *suprema lex* (the highest law).[1] But this good, as they thought at that time, is indissolubly connected with laws which are definite, unchanging, equally good for all those beings " endowed with feeling and reason ". These laws which were so passionately desired, which they invoked and which

[1] By the way, the *populus* (people) whose *salus* (good) was desired did not always mean the toiling and producing people. According to Voltaire the human race could not exist if there were not an " immense number of useful people who own nothing " . . . " they make use of people who have only their arms and goodwill . . . they grant them the freedom to sell their labour to those who pay best for it ". (Dictionnaire philosophique, arts. " *Egalité* ", " *Propriété* ".)

were the ideal expressions of the social and political aims of the bourgeoisie, were called natural laws. And since the psychological origin of the thoughts which made these laws desirable was not clear and even, the logical origin of these thoughts was forgotten, they declared, like Diderot in the article quoted above, that their essence was independent of interests. This brought the philosophers back again almost to those same innate ideas which had had such a bad reputation ever since the time of Locke.

" There exist no innate practical principles." Nature has not put a single idea into our soul. Locke said this, adding that every sect considers those principles innate which are in accordance with its faith. The philosophers got no further. The recognition of the existence of innate ideas would have been for them equal to their submission to these despised " principles " of a " sect ", of the supporters of the past. Nature has inscribed nothing in our soul. Therefore outworn institutions and outworn morality do not owe their existence to nature. But nevertheless there does exist a natural, universal and absolute law which can be discovered by reason with the assistance of experience. But reason then was on the side of the philosophers. Consequently nature had to express herself in favour of the aims of the philosophers. " Innate principles " were therefore " the past " which had to be destroyed; natural law was the future to which the innovators appealed. They did not renounce dogmatism. They merely stretched its limits in order to make a path for the bourgeoisie. The views of Helvétius were a threat to this new dogmatism. So the majority of " philosophers " did not recognize them. But this did not stop him from being the most consistent of Locke's pupils. The view, so widespread in the 18th century, that the world is ruled by public opinion was no less of a threat to his opinions. We have already seen that, according to him, people's opinions are dictated by their interests; we have also seen that these interests are not dependent upon human will (remember the case of the savages who killed off their old people because of economic necessity). " The progress of education ", by the help of which the philosophers thought to explain all historical movement, instead of explaining anything in its turn demanded explanation. The finding of such an explanation would have meant a real revolution in the sphere of " philosophy ". Evidently Helvétius suspected the consequences of such a revolution. He recognises that in studying the path of development of the human soul there often creeps into his mind the suspicion that " Everything in nature is fulfilled and acts by itself " and that " The perfection of the arts and sciences may be less the work of a genius than of time and necessity." " The similar " progress of science in all countries appeared to him to confirm this view. " If all nations, according to Hume's remark, really first begin by writing good poetry and only after this pass to good prose, then this constant progress of the human reason seems to me to be the consequence of some general and unclear cause ".[1] From all that the reader knows concerning our philosopher's historical views such language must without doubt seem to him very cautious and undecided. But it is precisely this complete undecisiveness which shows how unclear were the conceptions which met together in the head of Helvétius with the words interest, people's needs, the sense of which seems so clear, and so unequivocable.

At the basis of laws and morals however strange they may seem to us, there always lies " a real or, at least an imagined benefit ". But what is an imagined benefit? What does it depend upon, to what does it owe its origin? Evidently it owes it to the opinion of people. Here we again fall into the vicious circle from which we wished to escape: opinion depends on interest, interest depends on opinion. And it is most remarkable that Helvétius could not help returning to this circle. Certainly, he knew how to connect the origin of the most different and fantastic laws, customs and opinions with the real needs of societies, but as a result of his analysis he was always left with a remnant which did not dissolve before his metaphysical reactives. This remnant was in the first place religion.

The essence of any religion is found in fear before an unseen force, in people's ignorance of the powers of nature. All primitive religions are like one another.

[1] " De l'Homme ", Section II, Chap. XXIII.

Whence comes this similarity? From the fact that nations which are in the same condition always have the same spirit, the same laws and the same character. "From the fact that people who are brought into motion by almost similar interests, who have to compare among themselves almost the same objects and who possess the same instrument of comparison, that is the same mind, must inevitably reach the same conclusions. From the fact that in general all proud persons . . . consider man to be the only favourite of heaven and the chief object of its cares ". And this pride compels people to believe in all the stupidities which charlatans invent for them. Open the Koran (for appearance' sake Helvétius only speaks of the " false religions "). It can be interpreted in a thousand ways. It is dark and incomprehensible. But so great is human blindness that to this very day this book crammed with lies and stupidity, this work in which God is drawn as a tyrant deserving of damnation, is considered as holy. Therefore the interest which creates religious lightness of credulity is the interest of vanity, the interest of prejudice. In place of explaining whence come peoples' sensations, he himself is only the expression of these sensations. " The benefit " of religion is merely an " imagined benefit ". The 18th century philosopher could have no other attitude towards the " vile " enemy of reason.

Once granted vanity and ignorance, those parents of fear, it is not hard to understand how the servants of religion strengthen and preserve their authority. " The first task of every religion which the priests assume is the lulling to sleep of man's striving for knowledge and his diversion from the investigation of any dogma the obvious stupidity of which could not escape him. To achieve this it is necessary to flatter men's passions so that they should desire and be interested in their own blindness. There is nothing easier for the bonzes ", etc. We see in the first place, that religious dogmas and customs are invented with conscious intention by a few cunning, greedy and bold charlatans : in the second place we see that the interest of the nations which should have explained to them, at least, the astonishing success of these charlatans, is often merely an " invented " interest of the blind who wish to lead the blind. It is obviously not a real interest, not the " need " which calls forth the appearance of all arts and science.

Everywhere where Helvétius explains his historical views he constantly, without noticing it himself, hesitates between these two diametrically opposite conceptions of interest. This is why he could not share the theory according to which the world is ruled by public opinion. In the one case he tells us that men owe their intelligence to the condition in which they find themselves; at another time it appears as clear as day to him that men owe their condition only to their intelligence. Now he says that " hunger brings about the rise of many arts, that the common needs are always pregnant with discoveries," i.e. that every more or less great discovery is only the integral of an infinite number of small discoveries; then he assures us in his controversy with Rousseau that " the art of agriculture, the invention of the ploughshare, of the plough and of forging, presuppose, consequently, immense knowledge in the sphere of mining, the art of building furnaces, mechanics and hydraulics ". So this time the spirit, science, is the source of discoveries and in the final analysis, " public opinion " determines the progress of humanity. Now Helvétius shows us how the laws, customs and tastes of a nation may be deduced from its " condition ", i.e. from the " arts ", from the productive forces which it possesses and from the economic relations which arise on their basis; then he declares: " Virtuous citizens depend upon the perfection of the laws, while the perfection of these same laws depends upon the progress of human reason." Now he represents tyrannical power as the inevitable consequence of continually growing inequality in the distribution of wealth, then he draws the following conclusion : " Despotism, that terrible misfortune of humanity, is most frequently the effect of national stupidity. Every nation begins with a free existence. To what cause should we attribute the loss of this freedom? To ignorance, to stupid trust in the ambitious. The ambitious man and the nation are the maiden and the lion in the well-known story. Having persuaded the lion to cut off his claws and saw away his teeth, the maiden hands him over to the hounds ". Although Helvétius set himself the task of everywhere seeking in history for interest as the " sole motive of men ", he returns to " public opinion ", which, while lending greater or less interest to objects, becomes in the last resort the absolute ruler of the world. " Imagined interest " is the hidden rock upon which his truly grandiose attempt at a materialist explanation of human development is wrecked. In history as in morality this problem has proved insoluble from the meta-physical point of view.

If " imagined interest " so often takes the place with Helvétius of real interest, with which he wished alone to deal, then we see that the same misfortune happens also with public interest, which yields place to the interest of the " powerful ". There can be no doubt that in any society divided into classes the interest of the powerful is always the master of the situation. How does Helvétius explain this indisputable fact? Sometimes he speaks of force, but most often he finds a refuge in " public opinion " since he feels that force explains nothing, because in many instances, if not always, it is on the side of the oppressed. The stupidity of the peoples makes them submit to tyrants, to " the idle rich ", to people who think only of themselves. One of the most brilliant representatives of the French bourgeoisie in the epoch of its prosperity, he neverthe-less does not suspect that in the historical life of every class of " the powerful " there comes a period when its

" private " interest is also the interest of the progressive movement and in this way of society as a whole. Helvétius was too much of a metaphysician to understand the dialectic of interests. Although he repeats that at the foundation of every law, however strange it may be, there always lies or lay a real interest of society, nevertheless he sees in the Middle Ages merely an epoch in which men were transformed into animals like Nebuchadnezzar; the laws of Feudalism appear to him to be " masterpieces of stupidity ".[1]

Real need leads to the discovery of useful arts. Every art, once it has appeared and begun to be applied with more or less speed and success, evokes the appearance of new " arts " in dependence upon the productive relations of the society in which it saw the light. The attention of Helvétius only dwells for a moment on this phenomenon of the " arts " which arise out of " real " needs and which engender new needs that are no less real and themselves engender in turn new and no less useful arts. He passes too quickly to the " pleasant arts " whose task is to amuse the wealthy and drive away their boredom. "No matter how many arts remain unknown to us, so long as there is love! " he exclaims. Perhaps so. Yet how many arts would be unknown but for the capitalist production of the most necessary objects!

But what is real need? For our philosopher it is

[1] Cf. his " Pensées et réflections ", in Vol. III of his " Œuvres complètes," Paris 1818, p. 314.

in the first place physiological need. But to satisfy their physiological needs people must produce definite objects, while the progress of this production causes the appearance of new needs, just as real as the first, but whose nature is no longer physiological. It is economic, since these needs are the consequence of the development of production and of the mutual relations into which people must enter among themselves with the progress of production. Helvétius points out some of these economic needs, but only some. The majority escape him. So for him the strongest motive force in the historical development of society is the multiplication of citizens, i.e. the increase in the number of mouths which have to be fed and of bodies which have to be clothed etc. The multiplication of citizens is the increase in the general sum of physiological needs. Helvétius does not take into account that the " multiplication of citizens " depends in its turn on the economic condition of society, though he makes a number of fairly clear remarks upon this question. But he is very far from sharing the clear and definite views on this question of his contemporary, Sir James Steuart, who in his " Enquiry into the Principles of Political Economy ", London, 1767, attributes the " multiplication " of citizens to " moral " i.e. social causes and already understands that the law of population which is natural to any society changes together with the mode of production prevailing at the given epoch. Nevertheless, the views of Helvétius do not contain such trivialities as those of Malthus.

In nature everything is fulfilled and acts of itself. This is the dialectical point of view. Helvétius only feels that this point of view is in science the most fruitful and correct. The cause of the " monotonous " progress of the human spirit remains for him " unclear ". Very often he no longer recalls it; he appeals to it accidentally. " In morals, as in physics," he says, " only something important excites our attention. For important phenomena serious causes are always presupposed. People wish to see the finger of God in the fall of states or in revolutions. But at the same time how many crusades were undertaken or postponed, how many revolutions were carried through or held back, how many wars begun or stopped thanks to the intrigues of some priest, of a woman or a minister. It is only because of the absence of memoirs that we cannot find everywhere the Duchess of Marlborough's glove ". This point of view is directly opposite to the point of view according to which " everything is fulfilled and acts of itself ".

" The law of life which, growing in a great oak tree, lifts up its shoots, pushes out its branches, thickens its trunk and makes it the lord of the forest, is also the law of the tree's doom." Helvétius is here again expressing himself as a dialectical critic who understands the stupidity of an abstract and absolute opposition of the useful and the harmful. Here he remembers again that every progress in evolution has its immanent and irrevocable laws. Starting from this point of view, he arrives at the conclusion that there exist no " specific remedies " against inequality in " position " which, when applied for a long period, would not inevitably bring ruin to any society. But this is not his final conclusion. Only under the " form of government as it exists in fact " do there exist no specific remedies against this evil. Under a more rational form many measures might be undertaken against it. What is this beneficial form of government? The one which will be discovered by reason, operating upon experience. Philosophy is able to solve completely " the problem of perfect and stable legislation ", which may, in so far as any nation is in question, become the source of its happiness. Perfect legislation does not destroy inequalities in position, but it prevents the appearance of their harmful consequences. In his quality of a philosopher, Helvétius explains to us in the form of " a moral catechism " " the dictates and principles of justice " " the benefit and truth "[1] of which are proved to us by everyday experience and which should serve as the basis of " perfect " legislation. In addition, he adds to his catechism a few other features of this legislation.

The book " On the Spirit " frightened the supporters of natural law. They saw in its author the opponent of this law. Their fear was only half justified. Among

---

[1] " De l'Homme ", Section X, Chap. VII.

them Helvétius was only the stray lamb who sooner or later must return to the familiar fold. He, who, it seemed, had left no place for natural law, who clearly considered the most stupid laws and customs reasonable, concluded with the statement that in their institutions nations approached the nearer to natural law, the greater the progress in their reason. In this way he corrected himself and came back to the fold of the philosophical church. Belief, holy, salutary belief in " reason ", is victorious over any other point of view. " The time has come for the man who is deaf to all theological contradictions to begin to listen only to the teaching of wisdom ! "—he exclaims. " We have awoken . . . from our immersion in sleep; the night of ignorance has passed; the day of science has dawned ".

Let us listen to the voice of " reason ", let us look at the " moral catechism " of its interpreter.

" *Question:* What makes the right of property so sacred and why do we find almost everywhere that out of it gods have been created under the name of Terminus? " [1]

" *Answer:* Because the support of property is the moral god of states; because it supports domestic peace and brings the rule of justice; because people unite only in order to guarantee their property; because justice which includes in itself almost all the virtues,

[1] Terminus was the ancient Roman God who protected boundaries.

156

consists in giving to each what belongs to him and, consequently, is reduced to the support of this right of property, and because, finally, the various laws are always merely the means of guaranteeing this right to citizens ".

" *Question:* Do there not exist among the various laws some which are called natural? "

" *Answer:* They are those laws, which, as I have already said, affect property and which are in force among almost all civilised nations and societies, since societies can only be formed with the assistance of these laws ".

" *Question:* What must a sovereign do who wishes to improve the science of legislation? "

" *Answer:* He must inspire men of genius to the study of this science and employ them in the solution of different problems ".

" *Question:* What will then take place? "

" *Answer:* Changing and still imperfect laws will cease to be so and become unchanging and holy ".

Enough! The Utopia of " perfect legislation " in Helvétius, as in Holbach and all the " philosophers " of the 18th century, is only a bourgeois Utopia. The few features characteristic of our author do not change its essence. We will only quote some of them in order to complete the portrait of a man whose moral physiognomy has so often been distorted by the ideologues of the ungrateful bourgeoisie.

In his perfect society Helvétius does not compel the workers to work for as long as is the case with us. " Wise laws," he says, " might without doubt produce the miracle of general happiness. All citizens have some property and, being prosperous, might, by working 7 or 8 hours, satisfy the needs of themselves and their families with the surplus. They would be as happy as it is possible to be. . . . If labour is considered an evil at all then this is only because in the majority of states the necessities of life are obtained only by excessive labour and in consequence of this the idea of labour evokes in the mind the idea of suffering ".[1] Fourier's entrancing work is only the development of this main thought of Helvétius, just as the 8 hour working day is only the solution by the proletariat of the problem posed by the bourgeois philosopher, with just this difference, that the proletariat, "fortunately", does not halt its movement at that.

Helvétius stands for public education. In his opinion there are many reasons which give it preference over private education. He only brings forward one of them, but it is quite sufficient. Only from public education can the appearance of patriots be expected. It alone is in a condition to connect the idea of personal happiness with the happiness of the nation in the consciousness of citizens. This is also the thought of a bourgeois philosopher, the realisation

[1] " De l'Homme ", Section VII, Chap. I-II.

158

of which will be carried through by the proletariat
which develops it in accordance with the needs of the
epoch.

But Helvétius himself, as we know, expected nothing from the proletariat. To whom did he wish to
entrust the realisation of his plan? Of course, to the
sage on the throne. But since man is the product of
his environment, and since moreover, the environment
around sovereigns is a very harmful one, then what
reasonable basis can we have for hoping for the
appearance of a sage on the throne? Our philosopher
sees very clearly that it is not easy to answer this
question. He finds an embarrassed refuge in the
theory of probabilities. "Why despair of the future
happiness of humanity if, in a more or less long period,
it is necessary, as the sages say, for all possibilities to
realise themselves? Who can be certain that the
truths here established will always be useless? It is
rare, but necessary, that within a given time a Penn
should be born, a Manco-Capac, who will give laws
to new societies. Let us then imagine, . . . that,
jealous of a new glory, such a man wished under the
title of Friend of Man, to consecrate his name to
posterity, and that, more occupied with the composition of his laws and the happiness of peoples
than with the aggrandisement of his own power, this
man desired that men should be happy and not
slaves, then undoubtedly . . . he would perceive in
the principles which I have established, the germ of

a new legislation more in conformity with human happiness ".[1]

In so far as the " philosophers " concerned themselves with the question of the influence of environment upon man they reduced the influence of this environment to the influence of " government ". Helvétius does not do this so decisively as the others. At one time he saw and declared perfectly clearly that the government, in its turn, was merely the product of social environment. He was able, more or less successfully, to deduce the civil, criminal and public law of his hypothetical island from the economic condition of this island. But as soon as ever he passes to the study of the development of " education ", i.e. of science and literature, he begins, as the reader will remember from the preceding exposition, to see only the influence of government. But the insuperable influence of government is a kind of *impasse* from which it is only possible to emerge by means of a miracle, that is by means of a government which shall suddenly decide to cure all the ills which it has brought on itself or which have been inflicted by previous governments. But Helvétius appeals to this miracle and to revive his own faith and the faith of his readers he takes refuge in an apparently limitless sphere, in the sphere of " probabilities ".

But a theory is not yet the truth. And least of all a theory which gives so little confidence as a theory of probabilities which may be realised in a more or less

[1] " De l'Homme ", Section VII, Chap. XXVI.

distant future. And so Helvétius, at least in so far as France is concerned, remains absolutely unbelieving. " My country," he says in the preface to his book " On Man ", " has at last fallen under the yoke of despotism. It will therefore never again give birth to a single eminent writer. . . . This nation will no longer be famous by the name of French; this humiliated nation is at present the object of Europe's contempt. No crisis of salvation will bring back its freedom. . . . Happiness is like the sciences, it is, so they say, a stranger on this earth. At present it is bending its path towards the north. Great sovereigns summon genius there and genius summons happiness. . . . To such sovereigns I dedicate this book ". It appears to us that it is precisely this disbelief, with its small counterweight in the belief in the sovereigns of the north, which allowed him to carry his analysis of moral and social phenomena further than the other " philosophers ". Holbach, like Voltaire, was an inexhaustible propagandist. He published a vast number of books wherein he actually always repeated the same thing. Helvétius wrote his book " On the Spirit "; his other book " On Man " is only an extended commentary on the first. The author did not wish to print it in his own lifetime.

" Whoever wishes to know the true principles of morality ", said our philosopher, " should, like me, turn to the principle of physical sensation and the needs of hunger, thirst, etc. in order to seek the causes which compel people when they have grown numerous to cultivate the earth, to unite in society and to conclude contracts with one another, the observance of which makes people just and the breaking of which makes them unjust ". So he undertook his analysis with the intention of finding the true principles of morality and at the same time of politics. In applying the principle of " physical sensation " he showed himself to be the most consistent and logical of the 18th century material-ists. By seeking in the " needs of hunger, thirst, etc." the causes of the historical movement of humanity, he set himself the task of finding a materialist explanation for these movements. From afar he saw many truths which have a much greater value than his plan of perfect legislation, than the unchanging and absolute " great truths " which he consecrated to the rulers of the " north ". He understood that a general " cause " must exist in human development. He himself did not know and could not know this cause since he lacked facts and the necessary method. For him it remained " hidden " and " unclear ". But this did not make him inconsolable. The Utopian consoled the phil-osopher in him. His chief aim was achieved: the principles of " perfect " legislation were worked out.

Two examples will be enough to show how Hel-vétius, in working out his Utopian plans, sometimes made use of the principle of physical sensation.

" I am not ", he says, " an enemy of theatrical performances, nor do I share M. Rousseau's views on this question. Theatrical performances are, no doubt, a pleasure. But, in the hands of a wise government, there is no pleasure which cannot become a principle productive of virtue, for which it would be the reward."[1]

And here again is a speech in defence of divorce. " If, moreover, it is true that the striving for change is, as they say, natural to human nature, then it might be possible to propose the possibility of change as a reward for merit; in this way one might try to make warriors more brave, officials more just, artisans more industrious and men of genius more jealous ". Divorce as a reward for " virtue "! What can be more amusing than this?

We know that if ever the principles of perfect legislation are realised, then the " changing " and still imperfect laws will cease to be so and will become unchanging. Society will then be in a stationary condition. What will be the consequences of such a condition? " Suppose that in each kind of Science and Art, men had compared among themselves all the objects and all the facts already known and that they had finally managed to discover all the relationships in them. Then, since there would be no more combinations to make, what is called the spirit (esprit) would cease to exist. Then everything would be Science, and the human spirit, forced to rest until the discovery of unknown facts allowed it to compare them once more and to combine them together, would be the worked

---

[1] " De l'Homme ", Section I, Chap. X. Note.

out mine which is allowed to rest until new veins are formed."[1]

So, this quiet, this exhaustion of the human spirit must, at least in so far as it affects the social relations of people, inevitably bring with it the realisation of the moral and political principles of Helvétius. Thus the ideal of this philosopher, the fanatical supporter of the progressive movement, is stagnation! Metaphysical materialism was only half revolutionary. Revolution for it was merely the means (and moreover only in view of the absence of peaceful means) of reaching once and for all the calm and longed for haven. . . . Two souls, alas, were alive in his breast, as was also the case with Faust and with the bourgeoisie, whose most advanced representatives were the materialists of the 18th century.

[1] " De l'Homme ", Section II, Chap. XV. Helvétius here calls the spirit " a complex of new ideas ", and Science the acquisition of ideas already known to humanity.

MARX

MARX

THE materialists of the 18th century were firmly convinced that they had succeeded in striking a fatal blow at idealism. The old metaphysic was dead and buried; " reason " wanted to hear nothing more of it. But matters soon assumed a different aspect. Even in the period of the " philosophers " the restoration of speculative philosophy was beginning in Germany and during the first four decades of the 19th century nobody would hear a word of materialism which, in its turn, was considered to be dead and buried. The materialist doctrine appeared for the whole philosophical and literary world as it appeared to Goethe, as " grey ", " gloomy " and " dead ": " people shuddered in front of it as before a spectre ".[1] Speculative philosophy was confident in its turn that its rival was forever defeated.

And it must be recognised that the latter had a great advantage over materialism. It studied things in their development, in their arising and dying away. If we

---

[1] See the 11th book of " Dichtung und Wahrheit " in which Goethe describes the impression which the " Système de la Nature " made on him.

examine things from precisely this last point of view, the method of thinking characteristic of the encyclopaedists,—the transformation of a phenomenon into a fossilised thing by abstracting it from all the inner processes of life, the nature and connection of which it is impossible to understand,—must be rejected. Hegel, the Titan of 19th century idealism, never ceased to fight against this method of thinking. For him " This metaphysic was not free or objective thinking. Instead of letting the object freely and spontaneously expound its own characteristics, metaphysic presupposed it readymade ".[1] The restored idealist philosophy sings a eulogy to the diametrically opposite method, the dialectical method, adopting it with astonishing success. Since we have already more than once had to mention this method and since we shall again have to concern ourselves with it, it will not be without its uses to characterise it in the actual words of Hegel, the master of idealist dialectic.

" It is customary to treat Dialectic as an adventitious art, which for very wantonness introduces confusion and a mere semblance of contradiction into definite notions. And in that light, the semblance is a nonentity, while the true reality is supposed to belong to the original dicta of understanding. Often, indeed, Dialectic is nothing more than a subjective see-saw of arguments pro and con, where the absence of stirring thought is disguised by the subtlety which gives birth

[1] " Encyklopädie," Paragraph 31.

to such arguments. But in its true and proper character, Dialectic is the very nature and essence of everything predicated by mere understanding,—the law of things and of the finite as a whole. Dialectic is different from ' Reflection '. In the first instance Reflection is that movement out beyond the isolated predicate of a thing which gives it some reference, and brings out its relativity, while still in other respects leaving it its isolation, validity. But by Dialectic is meant the indwelling tendency outwards by which the onesidedness and limitation of the predicates of understanding is seen in its true light, and shown to be the negation of them. For anything to be finite is just to suppress itself and put itself aside. Thus understood the Dialectic principle constitutes the life and soul of scientific progress, the dynamic which alone gives immanent connection and necessity to the body of science; and, in a word, is seen to constitute the real and true, as opposed to the external, exaltation above the finite ".

Everything about us can serve as an example of dialectic. " At this moment the planet stands in this spot, but implicitly it is the possibility of being in another spot; and that possibility of being otherwise the planet brings into existence by moving . . . To illustrate the presence of Dialectic in the spiritual world, especially in the provinces of law and morality, we have only to recollect how general experience shows us the extreme of one state or action suddenly shifting into its opposite: a Dialectic which is recognised in many ways in common proverbs. Thus *Summum jus summa injuria*: which means, that to drive an abstract right to its extremity is to do a wrong ".[1]

The metaphysical method of the French materialists is in the same relation to the dialectical method of German idealism as lower mathematics to higher. In lower mathematics conceptions are strictly limited and separated from one another as though by an " abyss ": a polygon is a polygon and nothing else: a circle is a circle and nothing else. But even in plane geometry we are compelled to apply the so-called method of limits which shakes our respected and immovable conceptions and in the most astonishing way brings them into proximity with one another. How can it be proved that the area of a circle is equal to the product of the circumference and half the radius? It is said: the difference between the area of a true polygon inscribed in a circle and the area of this circle can be made an arbitrarily small quantity on condition that the number of its sides is sufficiently increased. If the area of the circle, the circumference, the diameter of a true polygon inscribed in a circle are consecutively known by a, p and r, then $a = p.\frac{1}{2}r$; whilst a and $p.\frac{1}{2}r$ are quantities which change together with the number of sides but are always equal between themselves; their limits will therefore also be equal. If we consecutively name the area, circumference and radius

[1] Ibid., Paragraph 81 and Appendix.

of a circle A, C and R, then A is the limit of a, C the limit of p, and R the limit of r, therefore $A = C . \frac{1}{2} R$. Thus the polygon is transformed into a circle; so the circle is examined in the process of its becoming. This already represents a remarkable revolution in mathematical conceptions. Higher analysis takes this revolution for its starting point. Differential calculus has to do with infinitely small quantities or, in Hegel's words, " it has to do with quantities which are in the process of disappearing, not before their disappearance, for then they would be finite quantities, and not after their disappearance, for then they would not exist ".[1]

However astonishing, however paradoxical this method may be, it renders innumerable services to mathematics and proves by this that it is the direct opposite of the *absurdum*, for which for a long time people were inclined to take it. The " philosophers " of the 18th century knew very well how to value its advantages: they occupied themselves a good deal with higher analysis. But those people who, like Condorcet, for example, splendidly applied this weapon in their calculations, would be very astonished if we told them that such a dialectical method may be applied in the study of all phenomena with which science is concerned, to whatever sphere they may belong. They would answer that human nature at least is as

[1] " Wissenschaft der Logik ", Nürnburg 1812, I, Band. I. Buch I, p. 42.

stable and eternal as are the rights and duties of people and citizens which arise from this nature. The German idealists had another view. Hegel declared " that there is nothing which is not becoming, which is not in an intermediate position between being and non-being ". So long as in geology the theory of catastrophes was maintained, the theory of unexpected revolutions which at one blow renewed the surface of the globe and destroyed the old species of animals and plants in order to make room for the appearance of new ones, the method of thinking was metaphysical. But when this theory was renounced and in its place was put the idea of the slow development of the earth's crust under the influence of forces acting on it at the present time, then the dialectical point of view was approached.

So long as in biology it was thought that species are unchanging, the method of thought was metaphysical. The French materialists maintained this view. Even when they tried to relinquish it they were constantly returning to it again. Modern biology has once for all renounced this view. The theory which bears Darwin's name is in essence a dialectical theory.

Here, however, the following remark is necessary. However healthy the reaction against the old metaphysical theories of science may have been, it did in its turn, create in people's minds a pitiable confusion. A tendency was observed to represent the new theories in the sense of the old expression: *natura non facit saltus*—nature makes no leaps,—and they fell into the other extreme. They began to draw attention only to the process of gradual quantitative change in the given phenomenon; its transition into another phenomenon remained absolutely uncomprehended. The old metaphysics was stood upon its head. Just as before, phenomena remained separated from one another by an impassable gap. And this metaphysic has become so firmly rooted in the heads of modern evolutionists that there are " sociologists " to-day who show a complete lack of understanding every time they are compelled in their investigations to deal with revolutions. In their opinion revolution cannot be combined with evolution. *Historia non facit saltus*—history makes no leaps. If in spite of such wisdom revolutions in history nevertheless take place, and even great revolutions, that does not in the least disturb them. They firmly cling to their theory. So much the worse for the revolutions which disturb their calm. They are considered as " maladies ". Dialectical idealism also condemned and fought against this frightful confusion of ideas. Hegel says in regard to the above mentioned expression, "It is said, *natura non facit saltus*; and ordinary imagination, when it has to conceive an arising or passing away, thinks it has conceived them (as was mentioned) when it imagined them, as a gradual emergence or disappearance. But we saw that the changes of Being were in general not only a transition of one magnitude into another, but a transition from the qualitative into the quantitative, and conversely: a process of becoming other which breaks off graduality and is qualitatively other as against the preceding Determinate Being. Water on being cooled does not little by little become hard, gradually reaching the consistence of ice after having passed through the consistency of a paste, but is suddenly hard; when it already has quite attained freezing point it may (if it stands still) be wholly liquid, and a slight shake brings it into the condition of hardness. The gradualness of arising is based upon the idea that that which arises is already, sensibly or otherwise, actually there, and is imperceptible only on account of its smallness; and the gradualness of vanishing on the idea that Not-being or the Other which is assuming its place equally is there, only not yet noticeable; there, not in the sense that the Other is contained in the Other which is there in itself, but that it is there as Determinate Being, only unnoticeable."[1]

Thus:

1. The essence of everything finite lies in the fact that it cancels itself and passes into its opposite. This change is realised with the assistance of each phenomenon's own nature: every phenomenon itself contains the forces which give birth to its opposite.

2. Gradual quantitative changes in the given content are finally transformed into qualitative differences. The moments of its transformation are the moments of

[1] " Logik ", Buch I, p. 313.

leap, of interruption in graduality. It is a great error to think that nature or history make no leaps.

These are the characteristic features of the dialectical outlook upon which it is necessary to dwell here.

The dialectical method in its application to social phenomena (we are only speaking of this aspect) brought about a complete revolution. It may be said without exaggeration that we owe to it the conception of the history of humanity as a process regulated by law. The materialist " philosophers " saw here only the conscious acts of more or less intelligent and virtuous, but mostly unintelligent and very unvirtuous, people. Dialectical idealism accepts the existence of necessity where at the first glance there is only to be seen the disorderly play of chance, only the endless struggle of individual passions and aims. Even Helvétius, who by his " supposition " that both in history and in nature everything " is fulfilled and acts of itself " (his own words) was already approaching the dialectical outlook, explained historical events only by the qualities of the individuals who held political power in their hands. In his opinion, Montesquieu in his book " Sur la grandeur et la décadence des Romains " was incorrect when he denied the fortunate circumstances which helped Rome. He said that Montesquieu " has fallen into the unhappy position, too common among men of learning, of wishing to explain away everything, and also into the error of the merely book-learned, who, forgetting humanity, too easily attribute constant views and uniform principles to all bodies, whereas it is often one man alone who directs at his will those grave multitudes known as senates ".[1] How different is this from Schelling's theory which declares that in history freedom (i.e. the conscious actions of persons) becomes necessity, and necessity—freedom.

Schelling considered the most important problem in philosophy to be the question: " If we are absolutely free, i.e. if we act consciously, how can it happen that anything unconscious should arise in us which we never desired and which the freedom presented of itself was never in a position to perform? "[2]

For Hegel " world history is progress in the consciousness of freedom,—a progress which we must understand in its necessity." He thinks, like Schelling, that " in world history, thanks to men's actions, something different takes place from what they aimed at and what they achieved, what they immediately knew and wished for; they act in accordance with their interests, but at the same time bring something else into action which is contained in these interests, but which is outside their consciousness and intention."[3]

It is clear that from this point of view it is not the

[1] Cf. " Pensées et réflections d'Helvétius ", in Vol. III of his " Œuvres complètes ", Paris 1818, p. 307.

[2] " Systeme des transcendentalen Idealismus ", Tübingen 1800, p. 426.

[3] " Vorlesungen über die Philosophie des Geschichte ", 9 Bd. der Hegelschen Werke, Wrgb. von Gans, p. 22, 30.

" opinion " of people which " rules the world ", that it is not here we must seek the clue to historical events. " Public opinion " is subject in its development to laws which change it with the same inevitability as they determine the movements of heavenly bodies. In this way the antinomy is solved with which the " philosophers " were continually in conflict.

1. Public opinion rules the world; it defines the mutual relations of the members of society; it creates the social environment.

2. Man is the product of social environment, his opinions are determined by the qualities of this environment.[1]

Legislation can do everything—so the " philosophers " were continually repeating and they were firmly convinced that the morals of every nation are dependent upon its legislation. On the other hand, they just as often repeated that the corruption of morals brought about the doom of ancient civilisation. Here we have yet another antinomy: 1. Legislation creates morals: 2. Morals create legislation. And in such antinomies lay, so to speak, the essence and the misfortune of philosophical thought in the 18th century which could not solve them without emancipating itself from them nor explain to itself the causes of the strange confusion into which it was continually falling.

Metaphysics examines and studies things separately and independently of one another. When it feels the

[1] Cf. the essay on Holbach.

need of reaching the conception of a continuum it examines things in their reciprocity. It comes to a standstill here and goes no further, nor can go further, since for it things remain separated from one another by a gap, so that it has no conception of their development which explains both their causes and the mutual relations existing between them.

Dialectical idealism passes over these limits which the metaphysicians could not cross. It examines both aspects of the relation of reciprocity not as " directly given ", but as " the moments of some third thing, of a higher thing which is a conception " ! For example, Hegel takes the manners and constitution of Sparta. " To make, for example, the manners of the Spartans the cause of their constitution and their constitution conversely the cause of their manners, may no doubt be in a way correct. But, as we have comprehended neither the manners nor the constitution of the nation, the result of such reflections can never be final or satisfactory. The satisfactory point will be reached only when these two, as well as all other, special aspects of Spartan life and Spartan history are seen to be founded in this notion."[1]

The French philosophers felt nothing but contempt or even hatred for the Middle Ages. For Helvétius feudalism was " a masterpiece of stupidity ". While being far from a romantic idealisation of the morals and institutions of the Middle Ages Hegel nevertheless

[1] " Encyklopädie ", I Teil, Paragraph 156, Zusatz.

considers this period an essential element in the development of humanity. Moreover, he already sees that the inner contradictions of mediaeval social life gave birth to modern society.

The French philosophers saw nothing in religion but a mass of superstitions which man owed to his own stupidity and the charlatanry of the priests and prophets. They only knew how to fight against religion. However useful this work may have been in its own time it in no way helped the scientific study of religion. Dialectical idealism prepared this study. It is only necessary to compare Strauss's " Life of Jesus " with Holbach's " Critical History of Jesus Christ " to see the immense step forward made in the philosophy of religion under the beneficial influence of Hegel's dialectical method.[1]

When the " philosophers " studied the history of philosophy they did it in order to extract arguments in favour of their own views or else in order to destroy the systems of their idealist predecessors. Hegel does not fight against the systems of his predecessors. He considers them as different stages in the development

[1] By the way, instead of reading Holbach's book the German reader can look at " Leben Jesu " of H. E. Paulus, Heidelberg 1828. Here we have the same point of view. Only the German encyclopaedist outdoes himself in order to glorify that against which the French philosopher fought passionately. Paulus examines the miracle of goodness and wisdom in the same personality who produced on Holbach the impression of an ignorant and wanton idler.

of a " single philosophy ". Every particular philosophy is the daughter of its own time and " in philosophy the latest birth of time is the result of all the systems that have preceded it and must include their principles; and so, if, on other grounds, it deserves the title of philosophy, will be the fullest, most comprehensive, and most adequate system of all."[1]

" Perfect legislation " was one of the favourite objects of the investigation of the philosophers. Each of them had his own Utopia. Dialectical idealism despised this kind of investigation. " A State," said Hegel, " is an individual totality, of which you cannot select any particular aspect, even although a supremely important one, such as its political constitution; and deliberate and decide respecting it in that isolated form. Not only is that constitution most intimately connected with and dependent on those other spiritual forces; but the form of the entire moral and intellectual individuality—comprising all the forces it embodies—is only a step in the development of the grand whole,—with its place preappointed in the process . . . (the constitution) is therefore no matter of choice, but is that form which is adapted to the spirit of the people."[2]

In a word, dialectical idealism looked upon the universe as an organic whole, " developing out of its conception of itself ". The knowledge of this whole, the discovery of the process of its development—this

---

[1] " Encyklopädie," Paragraph 13.
[2] " Philosophie der Geschichte ", p. 50-51.

was the task which philosophy set itself to solve. A task that was noble, mighty and worthy of astonishment! The philosophy which set itself this task could appear to no-one as " grey " or " dead ". Quite the reverse! It delighted everybody by the fullness of its life, by the unsurpassable strength of its movement, by the beauty of its brilliant colours. And nevertheless the noble effort of idealist dialectical philosophy remained unrealised; it did not realise and could not realise it. Having given invaluable services to the human spirit, German idealism declined, as though to give a new proof of its own theory and to show by its own example also that " everything finite consists in the fact that it cancels itself and passes into its opposite ". Ten years after Hegel's death materialism again appeared in the arena of philosophical development and up to the present has not ceased to maintain its victory over its old antagonists.

What is this conception, this absolute idea, this world spirit, concerning which German speculative philosophy has talked endlessly? Is there a means of knowing this secret essence of which they thought that it gives life and movement to everything?

Yes! There is such a means and a very simple one. It is only necessary to examine it more attentively. You only need to do this and at once a most remarkable transformation takes place. This absolute idea so irresistible in its movement, so rich and fruitful, the mother of everything which was, is and will be in the coming centuries, at once becomes pale, immobile, appears a pure abstraction and very far from being able to explain anything at all, humbly demands some explanation of itself. *Sic, transit gloria . . . ideae* (thus passes the glory of the idea).

The absolute idea with all its immanent laws is merely the personification of our process of thinking. He who appeals to this idea in order to explain the phenomena of nature or of social evolution leaves the real ground of actuality and enters the kingdom of shadows. This is exactly what happened with the German idealists.

In a book which appeared at Frankfurt on Maine in 1845 and was written by two people who became famous in the second half of the 19th century, we find a remarkable exposure of " the secret of speculative constructions."

" When, operating on the realities of apples, pears, strawberries, almonds, I form a general idea of fruit; when, going further, I imagine that my abstract idea, drawn from real fruits, that is to say, fruit, is an entity which exists outside me and even constitutes the real entity of the apple, or the pear, I am stating, in speculative language, that fruit is the substance of the pear, the apple, the almond, etc. I say then that what is essential in the pear or the apple is not that it is pear or apple. What is essential in them is not their real being, concrete and sensually perceptible, but the abstract entity which I have abstracted out of them and which I have substituted for them, the entity of my imagination, fruit. I declare apple, pear, almond etc. to be simply forms of existence of fruit. Certainly, my final judgement, supported by its external senses, distinguishes an apple from a pear and a pear from an almond. But my speculative reason declares that this sensible difference is inessential and indifferent. It sees the same element in the apple as in the pear, and in a pear the same element as in an almond, that is, fruit. Real and particular fruits are nothing but apparent fruits of which the substance, fruit, is the real essence."

But German speculative philosophy did not really stand on the point of view of substance. " Absolute substance," Hegel says, " is truth, but it is not yet the whole truth. It must be understood as active, alive of itself, and is therefore determined as spirit." Let us see how this higher and truer point of view is reached.

" If the apple, pear, almond, strawberry etc., are in reality only substance, fruit, how is it that fruit appears to me now under the aspect of apple, now under the aspect of pear, etc? Whence comes this appearance of diversity, so manifestly contrary to my speculative conception of unity, of substance, of fruit? The reason is, the speculative philosopher replies, that fruit is not a lifeless entity, without distinctive characteristics, motionless, but an entity endowed with life, with distinctive characteristics, with motion. The differences in ordinary, real fruits are of no account to my sensible intelligence, but they are of account to fruit itself, to speculative reason. The different ' profane ' fruits are different manifestations of the ' single fruit,' are crystallisations produced by fruit itself. In this way, for example, in an apple or pear, fruit assumes the appearance of apple or pear. It is therefore impossible to say, as is done when one adopts the point of view of substance, pear is fruit, almond is fruit. On the contrary, one should say : fruit presents itself as apple, fruit presents itself as pear, fruit presents itself as almond, and the differences distinguishing apple, pear, almond, are the differences of fruit in general, and they make particular fruits out of the different members in the vital process of fruit. Fruit is therefore no longer a unity without content or difference. It is unity in so far as it is generality, in so far as it is the totality of fruits which form an organically distributed series." . . . " We see that while the Christian religion knows only a simple incarnation of God, speculative philosophy has as many incarnations as there are things. In this way it here possesses, in each fruit, an incarnation of the substance, of absolute fruit. For speculative philosophy, therefore, the chief interest lies in producing the existence of real fruits and in declaring in a mysterious fashion that there are apples, pears, almonds etc. . . . The speculative philosopher, it goes without saying, can only accomplish this continuous creation by putting forward as his own invention, properties recognised by everyone as belonging really to apple, pear etc.; by giving the names of real things to what abstract reason can alone create, that is to abstract, rational formulas; by declaring, in short, that his own activity, by which he passes from the idea apple to the idea pear, is the actual activity of the absolute subject, fruit."[1]

This materialist criticism of idealism is as sharp as it is just. " The absolute idea ", the spirit, of German speculative philosophy was merely an abstraction, but an abstraction about which it is thought that in the final resort it solves the deepest problems of science, can be nothing but harmful for the progress of science. And if the thinkers who appealed to this abstraction rendered great services to human thought, they did it not thanks to, but in spite of, this abstraction, in so far as it did not hinder them from studying the real movement of things. Thus, in Schelling's " Natural Philosophy ", we can find some very interesting remarks. Schelling possessed great knowledge in the sphere of natural science. But for him " the material universe " is merely " the revealed world of ideas." It may be that he was not contradicting himself when he declared that " magnetism " is a general act of inspiration, the penetration, " of the Single into the Many, of the Conception into Diversity " and that " the same transformation of the subjective into the objective, which in the ideal . . . is self consciousness, here appears expressed in being." But does this bring us a single

[1] " Die heilige Familie ", p. 80-84.

185

step forward in the knowledge of the phenomena of magnetism or in understanding its nature? We have not only not moved forward, but we incur the danger of denying real facts for the sake of a theory which may appear to us more or less clever, but in any case is absolutely arbitrary.

The same may also be said about the history of humanity. Sir Alexander Grant has said that Hegel's " borrowings in his ' History of Philosophy ' are equal to Shakespeare's borrowings in the sphere of poetry, i.e. are almost inevitable." In certain respects the study of Hegel's philosophy of history, as also of his aesthetic, his philosophy of law and his logic, is essential at the present time. But it is not his idealistic point of view which gives their value to these works. On the contrary, this point of view is absolutely fruitless and fruitful only in giving birth to confusion. For example, Hegel with a skill which would do honour to a specialist describes the influence of geographical environment on the historical development of human societies. But does he really succeed in explaining anything when he says that " the definite spirit of a nation, since it is real and its freedom exists from nature, has, thanks to the latter, a particular geographical and climatic stamp "? Or—if we take the example which he himself used—he certainly does not bring us one step nearer to understanding the history of Sparta when he tells us that the manners and constitution of this country were merely moments in the evolution of a conception. It is of course true that the point of view of the " French philosophers " against whom he brings this example (the point of view of reciprocity which was the insurmountable barrier of their most successful investigations) is absolutely inadequate. But it is also inadequate to renounce this point of view. It is necessary also to show in what degree the conception can be the hidden spring of a social movement. And Hegel not only never could answer this natural question but, it appears, he himself was very little satisfied with the light which this conception apparently threw upon the history of humanity. He feels the need to stand on firm ground and studies attentively social relationships. And behold, he concludes by categorically telling us that " Lacedaemonia fell . . . chiefly as the result of the inequality of property." It is true that there is not a scrap of absolute idealism concealed behind this truth.[1]

Imagine that someone explains to us with astonishing clarity the mechanism of the movements of animals. Then with no less astonishing seriousness he adds that the most important hidden cause of all these movements is to be found in the shadows cast by moving bodies. This man is an " absolute " idealist. Perhaps for a short time we shall maintain the view of this idealist but I hope that, finally, we shall master the

[1] For other examples of this kind we refer the reader to our article " Sixty years since Hegel's Death." " Neue Zeit " 1891-1892, Nos. 7, 8 and 9.

science of mechanics and say, " good-bye for ever " to the " philosophy of mechanics ".

That at least, is how the various pupils of Hegel acted. They knew splendidly how to estimate the advantages of the great thinker's method, but they themselves stood on the materialist point of view. The quotations given above from " The Holy Family " are enough to show how determined and merciless was their criticism of idealist, speculative philosophy.

The dialectical method is the most characteristic feature of materialism. Herein lies its essential difference from the old, metaphysical materialism of the 18th century. We may judge, therefore, the extent of the depth and seriousness of those historians of literature and philosophy who were unable to observe this difference. The late Lange divides his " History of Materialism " into two parts, Materialism before, and after, Kant.

To anyone not blinded by the spirit of the schoolman or mere routine, another division naturally suggests itself, materialism after Hegel became something quite different from what it was before him. But could anything different have been expected? To judge the influence of 19th century idealism upon the development of materialism, it is necessary first of all to get clear upon what the latter has become in our day. But this is just what Lange never did. Although he speaks in his book about everybody and everything, even about nonentities like Heinrich Czolbe, he does

not have a single word to say about dialectical material·
ism. The learned historian of materialism did not even
suspect that there were materialists in his time who were
remarkable in quite other respects than Messieurs
Vogt, Moleschott and company.[1]

The ease with which dialectical materialism over-
came idealism must appear incomprehensible to anyone
who does not have a clear understanding of the main
question dividing the materialists from the idealists.
When starting off with dualistic prejudices things are
generally represented as though there are two completely different substances in man, on the one hand,
the body, matter, and on the other, the soul, spirit.
Without knowing, and often even without asking the
question as to what is the influence of one of these
substances upon the other, it is at the same time declared
with aplomb that it would be onesided to explain

---

[1] In this respect Lange in general followed the views and
habits of all learned authors in " good society ". Hettner, in
his turn, many times compared the doctrine of Diderot with
the doctrine of the modern materialists. But who is the
representative of the modern materialists in his eyes? Moleschott. Hettner knows so little about the present situation of
materialism that he thinks he is stating something deep when
he says: " Materialism in its moral teaching has so far not risen
above these wretched efforts (i.e. the efforts of the 18th century
materialists). If materialism wishes to give proof of its vitality
then its next and most important task must be the fashioning
of a moral teaching." (" Literaturgeschichte des XVIII. Jahrhunderts.") The honourable gentleman has remembered
rather late!

phenomena by means of one of these two substances. Such thinkers proclaim their pretended superiority over both extremes with great self-satisfaction and proudly state that they are neither idealists nor materialists. But however respectable this mode of examining philosophical questions may be in age, it is, in essence, only worthy of philistines. Philosophy could never be satisfied by such " manysidedness ", on the contrary it has tried to emancipate itself from the dualism so dear to eclectic minds. The most outstanding philosophical systems have always been monistic, i.e. spirit and matter have been for them merely two classes of phenomena, the cause of which is indivisibly one and the same. We have already seen that for the French materialists " the capacity of sensation " was one of the qualities of matter. Nature for Hegel was the " other-being " of the absolute idea. This " other-being " is to a certain degree the Fall of the idea; Nature is created by spirit, it only exists by force of its higher love. But this pretended Fall in no wise excludes the substantial identity of nature and spirit. Quite the contrary. It presupposes such an identity. . . . Hegel's absolute spirit is not the limited spirit of the philosophy of limited minds. Hegel knew splendidly how to laugh at those who saw two different substances in matter and spirit, " as mutually impenetrable as every matter in relation to other matter, and penetrating one another's pores in their mutual non-being, like Epicurus who set apart for the gods a dwelling in the pores of the cosmos, but with absolute consistency allowing them nothing in common with the world."

In spite of his hostile attitude towards materialism, Hegel valued its monistic tendency.[1] But in so far as we stand on this monistic point of view experience itself must decide which of the two theories, materialism or idealism, best explains the phenomena which we encounter in studying nature or human societies. And it is not difficult to be convinced that even in the sphere of psychology, a science which deals with facts that may be called primarily phenomena of the spirit, we work with greater success when we accept nature as our starting point, and examine the manifestations of the spirit as necessary consequences of the movement of matter. " Surely," says the agnostic Huxley, " no one who is cognizant of the facts of the case nowadays doubts that the roots of psychology lie in the physiology of the nervous system. What we call the operations of the mind are functions of the brain, and the materials of consciousness are products of cerebral activity. Cabanis may have made use of crude and misleading

[1] " Yet we must nevertheless recognise for materialism a desire full of enthusiasm to pass beyond the limits of two worlds having a similarly independent, substantial existence and of duàlism accepted as truth and destroy the isolation of primal unity." (" Encyklopädie ", III Teil, p. 389. Zusatz.) Let us remark in passing that in his " History of Philosophy ", Hegel gave in a few words a more correct estimate of French materialism and such people as Helvétius than is given by the professional historians of materialism.

phraseology, when he said that the brain secretes thought as the liver secretes bile; but the conception that that much abused phrase embodies is, nevertheless, far more consistent with fact than the popular notion that the mind is a metaphysical entity seated in the head, but as independent of the brain as the telegraph operator is of his instrument."[1] In the sphere of the social sciences understood in the wide sense of the word, idealism, as we have already pointed out, repeatedly reached a consciousness of its own incapacity and sought a purely materialist explanation of historical facts.

Let us once more emphasise that the great philosophical revolution which took place in Germany in the fifth decade of the 19th century was greatly helped in its foundation by the monistic character of German idealism. Robert Flint says " It is, in fact, the case that Hegelianism, although the most elaborate of all idealistic systems, presents only the feeblest of barriers even to materialism." This is perfectly true, except that Flint should have said " because ", instead of " although ".

This same Flint is correct when he continues, " it is true that thought is placed by it before matter, and that matter is represented as a stage of the process of thought; but since the thought which is placed before

---

[1] " Hume ". It would be correct to say that agnosticism is in spite of everything simply cowardly materialism attempting to observe good form.

matter is unconscious thought—thought which is neither subject nor object, which is therefore not real thought, nor even so much as a ghost, or a fantasm of thought—matter is still the first reality, the first actual existence, and the power in matter, the tendency in it to rise above itself, the root and basis of spirit, subjective, objective and absolute."[1] It is easy to understand how much this inconsistency inevitable for idealism facilitated the philosophical revolution about which we are speaking here. This inconsistency makes itself particularly felt in the philosophy of history. " Hegel is guilty of a double deficiency. He declares philosophy is the existence of the absolute spirit, but at the same time refrains from recognising the real philosophising individual as absolute spirit; secondly, it is only in appearance that he has history created by the absolute spirit as such. In fact, since the absolute spirit only becomes conscious *post festum* in philosophy taken as creative spirit, his construction of history only exists in the consciousness, opinion and representation of the philosopher, in the speculative imagination." These lines are from the founder of modern dialectic materialism, Karl Marx.[2]

The importance of the philosophical revolution carried out by this man of genius was expressed by him in a few words. " My own dialectical method

[1] " Philosophy of History in France and Germany," Edinburgh and London, 1874, p. 503.

[2] " Die heilige Familie," p. 127.

is not only fundamentally different from the Hegelian dialectical method, but is its direct opposite. For Hegel the thought process (which he actually transforms into an independent subject, giving to it the name of ' idea ') is the demiurge of the real; and for him the real is only the outward manifestation of the idea. In my view, on the other hand, the ideal is nothing other than the material, when it has been transposed and translated inside the human head."[1]

Before outlining the results at which Marx arrived by the help of this method we will make a rapid review of the tendencies which became marked in French historical science in the epoch of the Restoration.

.   .   .   .

The French " philosophers " were convinced that public opinion rules the world. When they remembered that according to their own sensualist theory man in all his opinions is the product of social environment, they declared that " everything depends on legislation ", supposing that this simple but instructive answer would dispose of the matter. Further, " legislation " is identified by them with state law, with the " government " of each given country. During the first decades of the 19th century this point of view became more and more rejected. It began to be asked whether it were not more correct to seek the roots of

[1] " Capital ", Volume I, Preface to second German edition, page 873.

political institutions in civil law.[1] And to this question an affirmative answer was given.

" The majority of writers, men of learning, historians or publicists, have sought to understand the state of society, the degree or kind of its civilisation, by the study of its political institutions. It would have been wiser first to study society itself in order to know and to understand its political institutions. Before they become a cause, the institutions are an effect. Society produces them before it is modified by them, and instead of seeking for the state of the people in the system or forms of government, the state of the people should first of all be examined in order to know what should and could have been the government. . . . Society, its composition, the manner and life of

[1] After the events of the close of the 18th and beginning of the 19th century it was no longer so easy to think that " public opinion rules the world ". These events have more than once shown the powerlessness of public opinion. " So many events decided by force, so many crimes justified by success, so many virtues condemned by disapproval, so much unhappiness abused by power, so many noble sentiments mocked, so many base calculations philosophically interpreted,—all this killed the hopes even of those people who most of all believed in the power of reason," wrote Madame de Staël in the VIII year of the French Republic. (" De la Littérature Considérée dans ses Rapports avec les Institutions Sociales," Vol. I, p. iv, Introduction.) By the way, all the Utopians in the epoch of the Restoration and of Louis Phillippe were convinced that public opinion rules the world. This is the basic principle of their philosophy of history. But we cannot here concern ourselves with the psychology of the Utopians.

individuals, in accordance with their social situation, the relations of the different classes of individuals, in short the condition of the people, surely this is the first question to demand the attention of the historian who wishes to know how the peoples lived and the publicist who wishes to know how they were governed. . . .[1]

Here we are already in the presence of a complete change in the historical views of the " philosophers ". But Guizot goes even further in his analysis of " The Composition of Society ". According to him, the condition of the people in all modern nations is closely connected with land relationships and therefore the study of their land relationships must precede the study of their civil state. " To understand political institutions it is necessary to know the various social conditions and their relationships. To understand the various social conditions, it is necessary to know the nature and relationships of property ".[2]

Guizot studies the history of France under the Merovingians and Carlovingians from this point of view. In his history of the English revolution he makes another step forward in picturing this event as an episode in the struggle of classes in modern society. It is no longer " land relations " but property relations

[1] " Essais sur l'Histoire de France ", 10th Edition, Paris 1860, p. 73, 74. The first edition of these essays appeared in 1822.

[2] Ibid., p. 75, 76.

in general which are now for him the basis of the political movement.

Augustin Thierry reached the same views. In his works on the history of England and France he considers the hidden cause of political events to be the development of society. He is very far from the opinion that public opinion moves the world. Public opinion for him is only a more or less adequate expression of social interests.

Here is an example of how he understood the English parliament's struggle against Charles I. " Every personage whose ancestors had been enrolled in the army of the Conquest left his castle to go into the royal camp and take the post to which his rank entitled him. The inhabitants of the towns and seaports went over in a crowd to the opposing camp. It might be said that the rallying cry of the two armies was on the one side, idleness and power, on the other, work and liberty : for the non-workers, the people who desired no other occupation in life but that of enjoyment without responsibility, enrolled, whatever class they belonged to, in the Royalist armies, where they went to defend interests similar to their own, while the families of the caste of the former conquerors who had been won over to industry joined the party of the Commons. It was for these positive interests that the war was kept up by both sides, the rest was only pretext or appearance. Those who engaged in the cause of the subjects were for the most part Presbyterians, that is to say that even in religion they desired no yoke. Those who supported the opposite cause were Episcopalians or Papists, that is to say they liked to find even in the forms of their worship the exercise of power and the chance to levy taxes on their fellow men."[1]

This is pretty clear, but it appears, perhaps, rather more clear than it really is. In fact, political revolutions are the consequence of the struggle of classes fighting for their positive economic interests. But what is the principle which gives this or that form to the economic interests of the class in question? What is the cause which gives birth to classes in society? Augustin Thierry speaks, it is true, of " industry ", but this conception remains confused with him, and in order to get out of his difficulty he recalls the invasion and conquest of England by the Normans. Thus the classes whose struggle caused the revolution owe their origin to the Conquest. " This has all taken place since the Conquest," he says, " the Conquest lies at the bottom of all this." But what is a conquest? Does it not bring us back again to the activity of " government " for which we have tried to find an explanation? And even setting this aside, the actual fact of a conquest can never explain the social con-

[1] " Œuvres complètes de Monsieur Augustin Thierry ", Vol. VI, 10th Ed., Paris 1866, p. 66. The article which we quote " Vues des révolutions d'Angleterre " was printed in 1817, i.e. a few years before the appearance of Guizot's " Essays ".

sequences of this conquest. Before the conquest of Gaul by the barbarians it was conquered by the Romans. But the social consequences of both these conquests were absolutely different. What is the cause of this? Undoubtedly the Gauls at the time of Cæsar were in a different situation from the Gauls in the 5th century, and it is just as undoubted that the Roman conquerors did not in any way resemble the " barbarian " conquerors, the Franks and Burgundians. But are not all these differences explained by other conquests? We might enumerate all the known and all the possible conquests; so long as we remained within the vicious circle we should reach every time the inevitable conclusion that there is something in the life of nations, some x, something unknown to which they owe their origin, their direction and their changes, " a force " of the nations themselves and of the different classes which exist within them. To put it briefly, it is clear that at the basis of this " force " something lies, and the question is reduced to the definition of the nature of this unknown.[1] Guizot moves within the

[1] Augustin Thierry owes his clearest historical views to Saint Simon. Saint Simon did a great deal to clarify the historical development of humanity. But he did not succeed in defining that x about which we speak in the text. For him human nature is in essence itself a sufficient cause for the development of humanity. He struck that same hidden shoal upon which the materialist philosophers of the 18th century were wrecked. We hope, by the way, to explain Saint Simon's views in a special essay.

circle of these contradictions. What do these "relations of property" owe their origin to among the nations about which Guizot speaks in his essays? To the actions of conquerors. "After the conquest the Franks became landowners; many of them settled on land which they had received or occupied . . . the absolute independence of their property as well as that of their person was their right; this independence had then hardly any other guarantee than the force of possession; but by using this force to defend it, he thought he was exercising his right."[1]

It is no less characteristic that for Guizot the civic life of people was only closely connected "with property relations" among the "modern nations".

Neither Mignet nor any other of the French historians of this period (and the French historians in this period belonged to different schools) were able to get out of the difficulty which halted Guizot and Augustin Thierry. They understood perfectly that the cause of the development of society must be sought for in its economic relations. They already knew that at the basis of political movements lie the economic interests which penetrate them. And after the great French Revolution, that epic struggle of the bourgeoisie against the nobility and clergy,[2] it was not difficult to understand this.

---

[1] Guizot, op. cit., p. 81, 83.
[2] The Liberal French historians in the epoch of the Restoration often spoke of the class struggle and, moreover, spoke of

But they were not in a condition to explain the origin of the economic structure of society and when they spoke on this theme they had recourse to conquest, returning to the point of view of the 18th century, since the conqueror is this same " legislator ", only appearing from without.

Thus Hegel, so to speak, arrived against his will at the conclusion that the solution of the puzzle of the historical fates of nations is in their social condition (in " property "). The French historians of the Restoration on their side, in order to explain the origin of development of different forms of " government ", deliberately had recourse to " positive interests " and to the economic condition. But neither the one nor the other, neither the idealist philosophers, nor the positivist historians, succeeded in solving the great problem which inevitably faced them; on what, in their turn, do the structure of society and property

it with great sympathy. They were never horrified of bloodshed. " So, I repeat, war, i.e., revolution, was essential," Thiers exclaims in one of his notes to his " History of the French Revolution " (Vol. I, p. 365, Ed. of 1834). " God gave justice to men only at the price of struggle." So long as the bourgeoisie had not yet completed its struggle against the aristocracy, the theoreticians of the bourgeoisie had no objection to the class struggle. The appearance of the proletariat on the historical scene to struggle against the bourgeoisie greatly changed the views of the above theoreticians. At present the point of view of the " class struggle " appears too " narrow " to them. *Tempora mutantur et nos mutumur in illis!* (Times change and we change with them.)

relations depend. And in so far as this great problem remains unsolved, in so far as the investigators in the sphere of what is called in France *les sciences morales et politiques* remained without any real scientific foundation, to that extent it was possible to oppose with complete justice mathematics and natural science as the only " exact " sciences, the sciences properly so-called to these pretended sciences.

The task of dialectical materialism was thus outlined beforehand. Philosophy which had rendered immense services to science in the past centuries, now had to emancipate social science from the labyrinth of its contradictions. In fulfilling this task philosophy might say: " I have done my work, I can depart ", since exact science must in the future make the hypotheses of philosophy useless.

The articles of Marx and Engels in the " Franco-German Annals " (Paris 1844), " The Holy Family " of the same authors, Engels' " Condition of the Working Class in England ", Marx's " Poverty of Philosophy ", Marx and Engels', " Manifesto of the Communist Party ", Marx's " Wage-Labour and Capital " already contain the outlines of the new conception of history splendidly formulated and clearly explained. But we find its systematic, though short explanation in Marx's book " The Critique of Political Economy " (Berlin 1859).

" In the social production which men carry on they enter into definite relations that are indispensable and independent of their will; these relations of production correspond to a definite stage of development of their material powers of production. The sum total of these relations of production constitutes the economic construction of society—the real foundation, on which rise legal and political superstructures and to which correspond definite forms of social consciousness. The mode of production in material life determines the general character of the social, political and spiritual processes of life. It is not the consciousness of men that determines their existence, but, on the contrary, their social existence determines their consciousness."[1]

What are relations of production? They are what in legal language are called property relations, the property relations about which Guizot and Hegel spoke. Marx's theory, by explaining the origin of these relations, answers in this way the very question which the representatives of science and philosophy were unable to answer before him.

Man, with his " opinion " and his " education " is the product of social environment, as the 18th century French materialists knew very well, though they often forgot it. The historical development " of public opinion ", as of the whole history of humanity, is a process subject to law, as the German idealists of the 19th century represented it to be. But this process is defined not by the qualities of the " world spirit ", as these idealists thought, but by the real conditions of

[1] " Critique of Political Economy ", p. 11.

man's existence. The forms of " government " about which the philosophers spoke so much have their roots in what Guizot briefly termed society and Hegel civic society. But the development of civic society is determined by the development of the productive forces which men have at their disposition. The Marxist conception of history which the ignorant consider narrow and onesided is really the legitimate product of the whole past development of historical ideas. It contains them all, in so far as they have real value, and gives them a firmer foundation than they ever had in any of their flourishing periods. It is, therefore, to borrow the expression we have already quoted from Hegel, the fullest, most comprehensive and most adequate of all.

The 18th century philosophers continually spoke of human nature as being destined to explain the history of humanity and to show the qualities which perfect legislation must possess. This thought lies at the bottom of all Utopias. The Utopians in their ideal constructions of a perfect legislation always started from arguments about human nature. The " conquest " of Augustin Thierry and Guizot in the same way brings us back again to human nature, i.e. to the more or less successfully imagined, more or less arbitrary nature of the conqueror.[1] But if human

[1] In his " Essays " mentioned above Guizot often refers definitely to the " needs of human nature ". In the second chapter of his book " On Property ", Thiers tries to show that

nature is something constant then it is clearly ridiculous
to wish to explain the historical fate of humanity by its
help, since this fate is by its nature changeable.   If it
is changeable then we should ask whence do these
changes come?   The German idealists, those masters
of logic, have already recognised that human nature
is a very unfortunate fiction.   They have established
the hidden mainspring of historical development outside man who, in their opinion, merely complies with
the irresistible impulses of this spring.   But for them
this motive force was a world spirit, i.e. one aspect of
human nature which had passed through the filter of
abstraction.   Marx's theory puts an end to all these
fictions, errors, and contradictions.   Acting by means
of his labour upon the nature which exists outside him,
man brings about changes in his own nature.   Consequently, human nature in its turn has a history and
in order to understand this history it is necessary to

"observation of human nature is the true measure which
should be followed in explaining the rights of man in society".
None of the " philosophers " of the 18th century could have
found any objection to such a " method ".   Moreover, the
Communist and Socialist Utopians against whom Thiers was
fighting could not have objected to it in any way.   This or
that conception of human nature always lay at the basis of
their arguments about social organisation.   In this respect the
point of view of the Utopians is in no way different from
the point of view of their antagonists.   It is perfectly clear
that this did not prevent them from " deducing " quite
other rights of man than those which Thiers, for example,
" deduced ".

understand how the influence of man on the nature existing outside him takes place.

Helvétius made an effort to explain the development of human societies by making men's physical demands their basis. This effort was doomed to failure since, strictly speaking, it is not the needs of man which should be taken into account but the ways and means of satisfying them.

An animal has the same physical needs as a man. But animals do not produce. They simply seize hold of objects the production of which is, so to say, the work of nature. In seizing hold of these objects they make use of their organs, teeth, tongue, limbs etc. Therefore the adaptation of animals to the natural environment surrounding them is carried out by the transformation of their organs by means of changes which take place in their anatomical structure. Things do not take place so simply with the animal who proudly calls himself Homo sapiens. " Man confronts nature as one of her own forces, setting in motion arms and legs, head and hands, in order to appropriate nature's productions in a form suitable to his own wants." He is a producer and uses tools in the process of production. " Leaving out of consideration the gathering of readymade means of subsistence, such as fruits, for which purpose man's own bodily organs suffice him as the instruments of labour, the object of which the worker takes direct control is not the subject matter of labour but the instrument of labour. Thus nature becomes an instrument of his activities, an instrument with which he supplements his own bodily organs, adding a cubic and more to his stature, scripture notwithstanding."[1] In consequence of this his struggle for existence is essentially different from the struggle of other animals for existence. The toolmaking animal adapts himself to the natural environment surrounding him by changing his artificial organs. In comparison with these changes the changes in his anatomical structure completely lose their significance. Thus, Darwin says that the Europeans who have settled in America very quickly experience a physical change. But in the opinion of Darwin himself these changes are " extremely unimportant. They are completely negligible in comparison with the innumerable changes experienced by the artificial organs of the Americans." Thus, in so far as man becomes a toolmaking animal he enters on a new phase of his development. His zoological development ends and his historical life begins.

Darwin disputes the view that there are no animals making use of tools. He cites many examples to prove the opposite. The chimpanzee in its natural state uses a stone to break fruits with a hard shell. In India elephants which have become domesticated break off the branches of trees and use them to drive away flies. This may all be perfectly true. But it should not be forgotten in the first place that quantitative changes are

[1] " Capital ", Vol. I, p. 169-171.

transformed into qualitative differences. The use of tools among animals is only encountered in its rudimentary form. The influence of tools on the life of animals is exceedingly slight. On the other hand, the use of tools has a decisive influence upon the manner of life of man. In this sense Marx says that " the use and the fabrication of instruments of labour, though we find their first beginnings among certain other animal species, is specifically characteristic of the human labour process ".[1]

It is perfectly clear that man does not make use of only mechanical means of labour. But Marx considers the latter are most characteristic of man. They comprise what he calls the osseous and muscular system of production. Its relics have the same importance for the estimation of economic and social formations which have died out as the relics of bones have for studying species of animals which have disappeared. " Economic epochs are distinguished not by the fact that production goes on but by how production goes on, and by what means of labour ". Historians and " sociologists " before Marx did not even suspect what a valuable means for the most important discoveries the technique of excavations could be. " Darwin has aroused our interest in the history of natural technology, that is to say in the origin of the organs of plants and animals as productive instruments utilised for the life purposes of these creatures. Does not the

[1] " Capital ", Vol. I, p. 117.

history of the origin of the productive organs of men in society, the organs which form the material basis of every kind of social organisation, deserve equal attention? Since, as Vico says, the essence of the distinction between human history and natural history is that the former is the work of man and the latter is not, would not the history of human technology be easier to write than the history of natural technology? ”[1]

The modern historians of culture talk willingly of a stone, bronze and iron age. This division of the prehistoric epoch proceeds from the chief materials serving for the production of weapons and utensils. These epochs are divided into different periods, as for example of rough and of polished stone. So the historians of culture do not quite close their eyes to the technology of excavations. Unfortunately, they are usually satisfied in this sphere by generalities which can only lead to similar generalities. They retire into this sphere merely thanks to the absence of other data, owing to the lack of anything better. But they leave it as soon as in history in the real sense of the word other data are found which appear more worthy of man and his reason. In this respect they continue in the main to follow the example of the 18th century, acting as Condorcet did a hundred years ago.

His famous work “ Esquisse d’un tableau historique des progrès de l’Esprit humain ” is begun by Condorcet with a description of the development of the produc-

[1] “ Capital ”, Vol. I, p. 392-393.

tive forces of primitive man from the rudest arts to the beginning of agriculture. He even goes so far as to say "that the art of making weapons, preparing food, of making the instruments necessary for this preparation, of preserving for a short time the means of nourishment, of creating their food reserves from them, was the first characteristic feature which began to distinguish human society from the societies of other animal breeds". At the same time he perfectly well understands that such an important "art" as agriculture must have an immense influence on the structure of society. But in his work the "Third Epoch" in human history already embraces "the progress of the agricultural nations to the invention of the alphabet", the fourth covers the progress of the human spirit in Greece up to the period of the division of the sciences in the century of Alexander. The fifth is characterised by the progress of science, etc. Without noticing it himself, Condorcet completely changes his principle of division and at once shows that in the beginning he only spoke about the development of productive forces because he could not do anything else. In exactly the same way it appears that the "progress" achieved in the sphere of production and material life of men in general is for him merely the measure of the progress of the spirit to which man owes everything, though it does nothing of the sort for him.

For Condorcet the means of production were the

consequence, and man's spiritual capacities, his spirit, the cause. So, as a metaphysician, he remained blind to the dialectic immanent in every process both in nature and society, by force of which every cause is only a cause after it has been a consequence, and every consequence becomes in its turn a cause. Since he observed the existence of this dialectic only where it appeared in the special form of the relation of reciprocity, he naturally preferred to take the bull by the horns and to appeal, in so far as he was able and in so far as he was not compelled to act otherwise, directly to the cause. The human spirit for him was the great motive force of historical development. Condorcet, like all the " philosophers " attributed to this spirit a " natural " tendency to progress. This of course, is a very superficial point of view, but we will be just. Have the contemporary historians of culture departed very far from Condorcet's point of view?[1]

It is as clear as day that the use of tools, of however

[1] By the way, in this respect the economists are no better than the historians of culture. What Michel Chevalier says about the progress achieved by the productivity of labour may serve as an example. " The productive force of man develops uninterruptedly throughout the consecutive epochs of civilisation. This development is one of the numerous and most attractive forms assumed by the progress of society ". (" Weltausstellung von 1867. Berichte des internationalen Jury, Einleitung von Michel Chevalier ", p. 21-22.) So what moves humanity forward is progress, a metaphysical essence which among its numerous other forms assumes the form of

developed a character, presupposes a relatively immense development of mental capacities. Much water had flowed before our simian-human ancestors reached such a degree of development of the " spirit." How did they reach it? We must not ask history but zoology about this. Darwin has answered for zoology. At least he has shown how the zoological evolution of man might bring him to the point which interests us. Certainly, the simian-human " spirit " in Darwin's hypothesis plays a fairly passive part, since in this hypothesis it is not a question of its apparently natural tendency towards progress, in so far as the latter is realised thanks to a combination of circumstances whose nature is elevated only to a very small degree. So according to Darwin, " man could not have attained his present dominant position in the world without the use of his hands, which are so admirably adapted to act in obedience to his will."[1] Helvétius also affirms this. He considered the progress of the extremities, *horribile dictu*, to be the cause of the progress of the brain, and, what is worse, he attributes the progress of the extremities not to the simian-human Spirit, but to the influence of natural environment.

the development of productive forces. This is the same old story of the idealistic personification of the processes of thought, of the product of abstraction; the same story of the shadows cast by moving bodies and called upon to explain to us the secret of the movement of these bodies.

[1] " The Descent of Man ", Vol. I, Chap. II.

However that may be, zoology transmits homo (man) to history already in possession of a capacity for invention and the use of the more primitive kinds of tool. Therefore to history's share falls only the investigation of the development of the artificial organs and the discovery of their influence on the development of the spirit, as has been done by zoology with regard to the natural organs. If the development of the latter was carried out under the influence of natural environment, then it is not hard to understand that the same thing has taken place also in regard to the artificial organs.

The inhabitants of a country which is without metal could not invent tools which were superior to stone tools. In order that man might train the horse, horned cattle, sheep, etc., i.e. the animals which have played a very important part in the development of his productive forces, he had to live in countries in which these animals, or rather their zoological ancestors, lived in a wild state. The art of navigation did not, of course, arise in the Steppes and so on. Consequently, natural environment, geographical environment, its poverty or richness have had an indisputable influence upon the development of industry. But in addition, the character of geographical environment has played another and more remarkable part in the history of culture.

" It is not the absolute fertility of the soil," says Marx, " but the multifariousness of its natural products which constitutes a natural foundation of the social division of labour, and, by changing the natural conditions of his environment, spurs man on to multiply his own needs, capacities, means of labour, and methods of labour. The need for the social control of a natural force, the need for economising it, appropriating it on a large scale, or taming it, the need for doing these things by the work of human hands, plays the most decisive part in the history of industry. Take, as an instance, hydraulic works in Egypt, Lombardy, Holland, etc. Irrigation in India, Persia, etc., is another instance. There, irrigation by means of artificial canals not only supplies the soil with the water indispensable to it, but also carries down to it in the shape of sediment from the hills, mineral fertiliser."[1] So man receives from his natural environment the material for the creation of his artificial organs by means of which he struggles with nature. The character of the natural environment determines the character of his productive activity, the character of his means of production. But the means of production just as inevitably determine the mutual relations of men in the process of production, as the armament of an army determines its whole organisation, all the mutual relations of the men of which it consists. But

[1] " Capital ", Vol. I, p. 557-8. " Therefore whilst the tropical continents boast wealth of nature, the temperate continents are most favourable for the development of man " (" Géographie physique comparée, considerée dans ses rapports avec l'histoire de l'humanité, par Arnold Guyot, Paris 1888 ").

the mutual relations of men in the social process of production in their turn determine the whole structure of society. Therefore the influence of natural environment on this structure is indisputable. The character of the natural environment determines the character of the social environment.

One example: " It was the need for being able to predict the rise and the fall of the waters of the Nile, which led to the study of astronomy in ancient Egypt, and thus established the dominion of the priestly caste as directors of agriculture ".[1]

But this is only one side of the matter. In order that we should not reach absolutely incorrect conclusions we must at the same time take the other side into account.

Productive relations are the consequence, productive forces, the cause. But the consequence becomes in its turn the cause, productive relations become a fresh source for the development of productive forces. This leads to a double result.

1. The mutual influence of productive relations and productive forces is the cause of the social movement which has its own logic and its own laws independent of natural environment.

Example: Private property at the primitive stages

[1] " Capital ", Vol. I, p. 558. In Asia as in Egypt " civilisations spring up in the alluvial plains which are easily tilled, and alike connect themselves with the great rivers." (Guyot, op. cit., p. 227; cf. Mechnikov, " La civilisation et les grandes fleuves historiques ", Paris, I, 889.)

of development is always the fruit of the labour of the property owner himself, as can be splendidly seen in the Russian village. But there necessarily comes a time when property assumes a character opposite to that which it formerly bore. It presupposes the labour of another, it becomes capitalist private property, as can equally well be observed every day in the Russian village. This phenomenon is the consequence of the immanent laws of the evolution of private property. All that natural environment can do in this respect is to accelerate this development by means of favourable conditions for the development of productive forces.

2. Since social evolution has its own peculiar logic independent of any kind of immediate influence of natural environment, it may happen that one and the same nation, living in one and the same country and preserving its physical qualities almost unchanged, will at different epochs of its history possess social and political institutions which resemble one another very little and are even absolutely opposed to one another. Because of this, attempts have been made to draw the conclusion that geographical environment has no influence on the history of humanity. But this is a completely incorrect conclusion.[1] The peoples who

---

[1] Voltaire also superficially denied the influence of geographical environment upon human societies, on which Montesquieu insisted. We have seen that Holbach, involved in contradictions thanks to his metaphysical method, now

inhabited England in the time of Cæsar experienced the influence of the same geographical environment as the English of Cromwell's day. But Cromwell's contemporaries possessed much greater productive forces than the peoples of the time of Cæsar. Geographical environment no longer exercised the same influence on them, since they themselves influenced their natural environment in an absolutely different way. England's productive forces in the 17th century were the fruit of the country's history, but in this history geographical environment had never ceased to exercise an influence, although in a very different way, upon the economic development of the country.

The mutual relations between social man and geographical environment are extraordinarily changeable. They change at every fresh step reached in the development of man's productive forces. In consequence of this the influence of geographical environment on social man leads to different results at different phases in the development of these forces. But there is nothing accidental in the change in the mutual relations between man and his place of habitation. In their consistency they form a process subject to law. In order to understand this process it is first necessary to remember that natural environment is an important

denied and now recognised this influence. In general the confusion which the metaphysicians of all tendencies have brought into the study of this question is undoubtedly one of the most remarkable illustrations of the weak side of this method.

factor in the historical development of humanity not thanks to its influence on human nature, but thanks to its influence on the development of productive forces.

" The temperature of this country (he is speaking of the temperate zone in Asia—G.P.), taking into account the character of the climate which does not experience great variations in accordance with the season of the year, is very close to the temperature of Spring. But in such a country men cannot be energetic and lively, they cannot support intense labour and effort. . . . If Asiatics are timid, distinguished by lack of manhood, not very warlike and with a milder character than Europeans, then the chief cause of this has to be sought in the character of the climate. Experiencing no great changes in temperature, in Asia the seasons of the year are almost indistinguishable from one another, and the transition from heat to cold is hardly noticeable there. In such a temperature the soul does not experience those lively shocks or the body those unexpected changes which naturally give man a more austere and strong character than when he lives in a temperature which is always the same, for rapid changes from one extreme to another inspire the spirit of man, dragging it out of its passive and careless condition ".

These lines were written very long ago, for they belong to Hippocrates.[1]   But even to-day there are not

[1] " Des airs, des eaux et des lieux ", trad., avec texte en regard, de Coray, Paris 1800, p. 76-85.

a few authors who go no further than he in their estimate of the influence of geographical environment on man : according to the place of habitation, such are the race, manners, science, philosophy, religion and, as the inevitable consequence of this, the social and political institutions.[1]

This appears very specious, but is in reality as superficial as all other attempts to explain the phenomena of social evolution by aid of this or that conception of human nature. Buckle rightly said that the influence of climate and soil on man are not direct but indirect. " But they have . . . originated the most important consequences in regard to the general organisation of society, and from them there have followed many of those large and conspicuous differences between nations, which are often ascribed to some fundamental difference in the various races into which mankind is

---

[1] " As Eastern Asia has a physical nature which belongs especially to itself, so it has a particular race of men—the Mongolian race . . . with it the melancholy temperament seems to prevail; the intellect moderate in range exercises itself upon details, but never rises to general ideas or the high speculations of science and philosophy. In genius, inventive, full of sagacity for the useful arts and the conveniences of life, the Mongolian, nevertheless, is incompetent to generalise their application. Wholly turned to the things of earth, the world of ideas, the spiritual world, seems closed to him. His whole philosophy and religion are reduced to a code of social morals limited to the expression of those principles of human conscience without the observance of which society is impossible ". (A. Guyot, op. cit., p. 269.)

divided ".[1]   Buckle willingly accepts John Stuart Mills' remark that " of all the common methods of ridding oneself of the examination of the consequences of social and moral influences on the human spirit the commonest is to attribute differences in behaviour and character to natural differences ".   This same Buckle

[1] " History of Civilisation in England ", Leipzig 1865, Vol. I, p. 36-37.   By the way, here as everywhere else, Buckle says nothing new.   Long before him the absolute idealist Hegel had succeeded better than he in estimating the influence of nature on man through the medium of productive forces and, in particular, through the medium of social organisation (cf., for example, " Vorlesungen über die Philosophie der Geschichte ", p. 99-100).   The acceptance of the direct influence of geographical environment on " human nature ", or, what is the same, on the nature of a race, is so far from any foundation that those writers who have admitted such an influence have been compelled to renounce their point of view at every step. Guyot, for example, adds to the lines we have quoted in the previous note: " The principal seat of the Mongolian race is the central tableland of Asia.   The roaming life, and the patriarchal form of their societies, are the necessary consequences of the sterile and arid Asia of the regions they inhabit ".   In the same way Hippocrates recognises that the Mongols' lack of bravery can be at least partly explained as " the consequence of the laws to which they are subjected " (op. cit., p. 86).   " The form of government of the Asiatic nations is monarchical," he says, " but governments are necessarily very cowardly where they are subject to kings " (op. cit., p. 117).   " A convincing proof in favour of what I say is found in the fact that in Asia even all the Greeks and barbarians are governed by their own laws without subjection to tyrants and therefore, working upon themselves, are very warlike people " (op. cit., p. 88).   This is not the whole truth, but it is at least an approximation to it.

in speaking of the influence of nature on the historical development of man falls into the identical mistakes against which he has warned others with such warmth and so correctly.

" Earthquakes and volcanic eruptions are more frequent and more destructive in Italy, and in the Spanish and Portuguese peninsula than in any of the other great countries; and it is precisely there that superstition is most rife, and the superstitious classes most powerful. Those were the countries where the clergy first established their authority, where the worst corruptions of Christianity took place, and where superstition has during the longest period retained the firmest hold."[1]

So, according to Buckle, the general character of the place of habitation not merely influences the intensity of the religious sentiment of the inhabitants, but also the social condition of the priesthood, i.e. the whole social structure of society. Nor is this all.

" Now it is remarkable, that all the greatest painters, and nearly all the greatest sculptors modern Europe has possessed, have been produced by the Italian and Spanish peninsulas. In regard to science, Italy has no doubt several men of conspicuous ability, but their numbers are out of all proportion small when compared with her artists and poets ".[2]

So here the physical qualities of a country have a

---

[1] Ibid., p. 113.
[2] Ibid., p. 114.

decisive influence on the development of the sciences and arts. The warmest supporters of the " vulgar " theory of races have never made bolder or less founded statements.

The scientific history of humanity's spiritual development still remains to be written in its entirety. So far we must be satisfied in this sphere with more or less clever hypotheses. But there are hypotheses and hypotheses. Buckle's hypotheses on the influence of nature do not stand criticism.

In fact ancient Greece was as famous for its thinkers as for its artists. Yet nature in Greece is hardly less majestic than in Italy or Spain. Even granting that its influence on the human imagination was stronger in Italy than in the country of Pericles, it is nevertheless sufficient to recall that " Greater Greece " included in fact South Italy and the neighbouring islands, which did not prevent it from giving birth to many thinkers.

The fine arts in modern Italy and Spain, as everywhere, have their history. The apex of Italian painting is to be found in a very short period extending over no more than fifty or sixty years.[1] The great period of painting in Spain also flourished for a short

[1] " In this short period of time there flourished the perfect artists : Leonardo da Vinci, Raphael, Michael Angelo, Andrea del Sarto, Fra Bartolomeo, Giorgione, Titian, Sebastian del Piombo, Correggio. This period of time was strictly limited. If we go beyond its limits in this or that direction we meet in the one case imperfect and in the other decadent art." (H. Taine, " Philosophie de l'Art ", 5th Ed., I, p. 126.)

time. It is quite impossible for us to dwell on the reasons why Italian painting flourished precisely at this period (from the last quarter of the 15th century to the first third of the 16th) and not in some other epoch, a century earlier or later, but we know quite well that nature in the Italian peninsula had absolutely nothing to do with it. Nature in the 15th century was exactly the same as in the 13th or 17th. But if a changing quantity alters, that does not take place because a constant one remains unchanged.

We may object to what Buckle has to say upon the influence and power of the clergy in Italy that it would be hard to find an example more contradictory of the essence of the argument which he is seeking to uphold. In the first place the role of the clergy in Catholic Italy has nothing in common with the role of the clergy in ancient Rome, although the physical characteristics of the country had undergone no remarkable changes in this period. In the second place, since the Catholic Church is an international organisation, it is evident that the Pope, the head of the " superstitious class ", owed the greater part of his power in Italy to causes which had nothing to do either with the physical characteristics of the country or of its own social structure.[1] Many times driven out by the population of Rome, the " Holy Father " was only able to

---

[1] Concerning the social causes giving birth to this international organisation of the priesthood see the first part of Karl Kautsky's excellent book " Thomas More and his Utopia ".

establish himself again in the eternal city thanks to the help of the transalpine States. The absolutely exceptional position of Rome as the home of the head of the Church was bound to exercise a strong influence upon the role of the clergy throughout Italy. But it should not be thought that the clergy in Italy was always more powerful than in other European countries, as Germany, for example. This would be a great mistake.[1]

The learned persons who have occupied themselves with the history of religion have been very inclined right up to the present day to seize upon racial qualities every time they meet a peculiarity in the religious doctrine of any nation, the origin of which is not easy to understand. Nevertheless they are forced, because of its obvious character, to declare the primitive identity of the religions of the savages and barbarians who inhabit localities of absolutely different character.[2]

They were forced in the same way to recognise the

[1] Long ago Saint Bernard advised Pope Eugene III to abandon the Romans and exchange Rome for the whole world (*Urbem pro orbe mutandum*).

[2] " We might quote an infinite number of examples of differences dependent upon the habitation and qualities of the race. But it is impossible to deduce from this any difference in principle. The religion of an uncivilised man is everywhere the same, no matter whether it develops in a ridiculously crude or splendidly poetic form. Everywhere we find naturalism, animism, belief in witches, fetishism or idol worship, sacrifices, presentiment of the continuation of life after death (the author whom we are quoting is a Christian—G.P.), faith in the continuation of the forms and relationships of real life beyond the

224

enormous influence of the manner of life and means of production of every nation on the character of its religious teaching.[1] Therefore science would only gain if it abandoned all wordy and " hypothetical " arguments about the direct influence of geographical environment upon this or that quality of the " human spirit " and began in the first place to try to define the role played by environment in the development of productive forces and through these forces in the whole social and spiritual, in short, in the historical development of nations.

grave, the cult of the dead and of the burial of the dead in accordance with this faith." (" Les Réligions des peuples non civilisés ", par A. Reville, Paris, 1833, II, p. 221-2.)

[1] " At the lowest stage stands the religion of the Australians who feed on roots, who, although they engage in hunting, show very little art in it, and the religion of the bushmen who to a large extent live by theft. Mild among the Hotentots and Kafirs who are chiefly engaged in stock breeding, religion is, on the contrary, bloodthirsty and harsh among certain warlike negro tribes, whilst among those nations who are chiefly engaged in industry and trade whilst not despising stock rearing and agriculture, divine worship has a more human and civilised character, while the spirit of trade is usually expressed in various kinds of cunning with regard to souls. The myths of the Polynesians at once disclose a people of agriculturists and fishermen." (Tiller, Text book in the " History of Religion ", translated from the Dutch by Maurice Berne, Paris 1880, p. 18.) " In a word it is beyond doubt that the cycle of festivals established by the laws of Jehovah was determined by agriculture, that common foundation of life and religion." We might bring forward any number of similar quotations each more typical than the last.

Let us go further.

" At a certain stage of their development, the material forces of production in society come in conflict with the existing relations of production, or—what is but a legal expression for the same things—with the property relations within which they had been at work before. From forms of development of the forces of production these relations turn into their fetters. Then comes the period of social revolution. With the change of the economic foundation the entire immense superstructure is more or less rapidly transformed. In considering such transformations the distinction should always be made between the material transformation and the economic conditions of production which can be determined with the precision of natural science, and the legal, political, religious, aesthetical or philosophic —in short ideological forms in which men become conscious of this conflict and fight it out. Just as our opinion of an individual is not based on what he thinks of himself, so can we not judge of such a period of transformation by its own consciousness; on the contrary, this consciousness must rather be explained from the conditions of material life, from the existing conflict between the social forces of production and the relations of production."[1]

Everything finite cancels itself, passes into its opposite. The reader sees that according to Marx the same thing also applies to both social and political institu-

[1] " Critique of Political Economy ", Preface p. 12.

tions. Every social institution is in the first place a " form of development " of productive forces. This, so to speak, is the best time of its life. It grows strong, develops and reaches its height. Instinctively people are attached to it and proclaim it " sacred " or " natural ". But gradually old age comes on, decline sets in. They begin to notice that not everything about this institution is as splendid as once they thought. They begin to struggle against it, declare it " an invention of the devil " or " against nature " and finally destroy it. This takes place because the productive forces of society are no longer what they once were; it takes place because they have already made a fresh step forward, thanks to which changes have taken place in the mutual relations of people and the social process of production. Gradual quantitative changes have been transformed into qualitative differences. The moments of these changes are moments of leaps, of a break in gradualness. This is that same dialectic which we know of from Hegel, but which is still not quite the same. In Marxist philosophy it has become transformed into the complete opposite of what it was with Hegel. For Hegel the dialectic of social life, as every dialectic of the finite in general, in the final resort has a mystic cause, the nature of the infinite, of the absolute spirit—with Marx it depends upon absolutely real causes, upon the development of the means of production which are at the disposition of society. *Mutatis mutandis* (with the necessary changes) Darwin reached the same point of view in order to explain " The Origin of Species ", and just as since Darwin's day it has no longer been necessary to appeal to the " innate tendencies " of organisms towards " progress " (tendencies the existence of which was admitted by Lamarck and Erasmus Darwin) in order to explain the development of species, just so to-day in the sphere of social science we no longer need to appeal to mystical " tendencies " of " the human spirit " in order to understand its " progress ". The character of men's life is for us sufficient to explain the character of their thoughts and feelings.

Fichte has complained bitterly that " it is easier to bring the majority of people to consider themselves as bits of lava in the moon than as themselves." Any good philistine of our day will also more easily recognise that he is " a bit of lava in the moon " than accept a theory according to which all his ideas, views and habits owe their origin to the economic relations of his time. He prefers to appeal to human freedom, to reason and to an endless number of other things no less splendid and worthy of respect. The good philistines do not even suspect when they grow indignant with Marx that this " limited " man merely solved the contradictions which had tormented science for almost a whole century.

Let us take an example. What is literature? Literature, the good philistines answer in chorus, is an expression of society. This splendid definition has only one deficiency,—it is so wordy that it expresses absolutely nothing.   In what degree does literature express society?   And in so far as society itself develops, how is social development expressed in literature?   What literary forms correspond to each phase of the historical development of humanity?   These inevitable and absolutely legitimate questions are, however, left unanswered by the above definition.   Since, moreover, literature is an expression of society, it is evidently necessary before speaking of the development of literature to make clear for oneself the laws of social development and the hidden forces of which this development is the consequence.   The reader will therefore see that the above definition has only a certain value in so far as it brings us face to face with the problem which already confronted the " philosophers " in Voltaire's time, as well as the historians and philosophers of the 19th century, that is with the problem, upon what in the last resort does social development depend?

Even the ancients knew very well that oratory, for example, depends to a definite degree upon the manners and political constitution of society (cf. the dialogue on orators attributed to Tacitus).   The authors of the last century (the 18th) were just as aware of this.   As we have shown in our preceding essays Helvétius more than once appealed to the condition of society in order to explain the origin of tendencies in aesthetic taste.   In 1800 appeared the book of Madame de Staël-Holstein: " De la littérature considérée dans ses rapports avec les institutions sociales " (Literature in its relations to social institutions). Under the restoration and Louis Phillippe, Villemains, Saint-Beuve and many others declared loudly that literary revolutions only arise as a consequence of social evolution. On the other bank of the Rhine, the great philosophers, examining literature and the fine arts, like everything else, in the process of becoming, had, in spite of their idealism, a clear conception of the close connection of every art with the social environment which gave birth to the artist.[1] Finally, in order not to accumulate these examples unnecessarily let us just mention that the outstanding critic and historian of literature, Taine, brought forward the following general rule as the main principle of his scientific aesthetics: " The great changes which take place in the relations between people, gradually produce corresponding changes in human thoughts." It would seem as though the problem was completely solved by this and the way clearly pointed

[1] To this place, for example, belongs what Hegel says of Dutch painting: " Satisfaction of the daily needs of life, even of the most ordinary and petty, with them proceeds from the fact that they have to win in hard struggle and the sweat of their brow what nature gives directly to other nations. . . . They are, on the other hand, a nation of fishermen, of sailors, of burghers and peasants, and as a result of this from the very beginning have learned to value in both great and small, in both necessary and useful, what they have won for themselves by energetic activity." (" Vorlesungen über die Aesthetik ", hrsg. von H. G. Hotho, II, p. 222; I, p. 217.)

out for the scientific history of literature and the fine arts. But nevertheless, strangely enough, we see that our modern historians of literature have no clearer idea of the spiritual development of humanity than their predecessors a hundred years ago. How can we explain this astonishing philosophical barrenness in these people who have as much diligence as learning?

The reason is not far to seek. But in order to understand it, it is first necessary to establish wherein lie the advantages and deficiencies of modern scientific aesthetics.

According to Taine " it is distinguished from the old by the fact that it has a historical and not a dogmatic character, i.e. that it does not establish dictates but states laws ". Excellent. But how can this aesthetics guide us in the study of literature and the different arts? How does it act in the investigation of laws? How does it examine a work of art?

In order to avoid any misunderstandings let us turn to Taine himself for this and allow him to speak.

Stating that a work of art is determined by the general condition of men's minds and the prevailing manners, and supporting this argument with historical examples he continues:

" In the different examples we have examined, you have first of all remarked a general condition, that is to say the universal presence of certain benefits and certain evils, a state of servitude or of liberty, a state of poverty or riches, a certain form of society, a certain kind of religion; the free, warlike and slave-owning city of Greece; oppression, invasion, feudal brigandage and exalted Christianity in the Middle Ages; the court in the 17th century; the enlightened industrial democracy of the 19th century; in short, a totality of circumstances to which men have to bow and to which they were subjected.

" This condition developed corresponding needs in them, distinct aptitudes, particular sentiments. . . .

" Now this group of sentiments, of needs and of constitutional aptitudes, when it is completely and brilliantly manifested in the same soul, forms a dominant personality, that is to say, the model which contemporaries surround with their admiration and sympathy : in Greece, the naked and finely bred youth, accomplished in all bodily exercises; in the Middle Ages, the ecstatic monk and amorous knight; in the 17th century, the perfect courtier; in our own day, the insatiable and melancholy Faust or Werther.

" But since this personality is the most interesting, the most important and the most visible, it is he whom the artists present to the public, now concentrated into a living figure when their art, like painting, sculpture, the novel, the epic and the theatre, is imitative; now dispersed into its elements when their art, like architecture and music, awakes emotions without creating persons. Their work, therefore, can all be expressed by saying that now they represent him, now they address themselves to him. They address him in Beethoven's symphonies and the rose windows of the cathedrals. They represent him in Meleager and the daughters of Niobe, in the Agamemnon and Achilles of Racine. In this way all art is dependent on him, since art as a whole applies only to pleasing him or expressing him.

" A general situation which excites definite tendencies and faculties; a dominant personality formed by the predominance of these tendencies and faculties; the sounds, forms, colours or words which give sensibility to this personality, or which are in accord with the tendencies and faculties of which he is made up, such are the four terms of the series. The first implies the second, which implies the third, and this the fourth; so that the slightest change in one of these terms, bringing a corresponding change in the preceding one, allows us to come down or to go up from one to another by pure reasoning. As far as I can judge, this formula leaves nothing outside of its limits."[1] In fact this " formula " leaves very important things outside its limits. One might have a few things to say concerning the argument accompanying this. For example, it would be perfectly just to state that in the Middle Ages there existed as " dominant personalities " not merely the exalted monk and the amorous knight.[2] It might

[1] " Philosophie de l'art ", 5 éd., Paris 1890, I, p. 116-119.
[2] Even if we do not mention here Folklore, or the poetry of the peasants and petty burghers, even the mediaeval warriors

also be declared that " in our time " not Faust and Werther alone inspire our arts.   But however that may be, Taine's " formula " brings us forward to a considerable degree in the comprehension of the history of art and tells us infinitely more than the wordy definition : " Literature is the expression of society ".   By using this formula, Taine has done a great deal for the history of the fine arts and literature.   But in reading his best books, his " Philosophy of Art " from which we have just quoted, his essay on Racine, his " History of English Literature ", you ask yourself, is this satisfactory?   Of course not!   In spite of all his talent, in spite of the indisputable advantages of his method, the author only gives us fragments which, even as such, leave much to be desired.   " The History of English Literature " is rather a series of brilliant characterisations than a history.   What Taine tells us about ancient Greece, about Italy in the epoch of the Renaissance, about the Netherlands, acquaints us with the chief features of the art of each one of these countries but in no way explains to us their historical origin, or explains it only to a very slight degree.   And it is necessary to observe that in this case it is not the author who is at fault, but his point of view, his conception of history.

In so far as the argument is put forward that the

were not always " amorous knights ". The hero of the famous song of Roland was " in love " only with his sword " Durandel ".

history of art is closely connected with the history of social environment, in so far as the opinion is expressed that every big change in men's relations calls forth a corresponding change in men's ideas—to this extent the necessity is recognised of first establishing the laws of the evolution of the social environment, of clearly understanding the causes which give birth to important changes in the relations of people in order that then the laws of the evolution of art may be correctly established. In a word, it is necessary to found " historical aesthetics " upon a scientific conception of the history of societies. Has Taine done this at all satisfactorily? No. A materialist in the sphere of the philosophy of art, he was an idealist in his conception of history. " Just as astronomy is in essence a problem in mechanics, and physiology a problem of chemistry, so history is a problem of psychology ".[1] He examines the social environment in which he constantly turns as a product of the human spirit. We consequently find in him the same contradiction which we encountered in the 18th century French materialists. Men's ideas owe their condition to their origin. Man's condition, in the last resort, owes its origin to men's ideas. So we ask the reader, is it easy to employ in aesthetics a historical method which has such confused and contradictory conceptions of history in general? Of course not. One may possess unusual abilities and

[1] " Histoire de la littérature anglaise ", 8 éd., introduct., p. iv-v.

still be very far from carrying out the tasks placed before one, being satisfied with an aesthetics which is only half historical.

The French philosophers in the 18th century thought they would explain the history of the arts and literature by appealing to the qualities of human nature. Humanity passes through the same phases of life as the separate individual,—childhood, youth, maturity, etc. The epic corresponds to childhood, rhetoric and the drama to youth, philosophy to maturity, etc.[1] We have already said in one of our previous essays that such a comparison is absolutely unfounded. We may add here that Taine's " historical " aesthetics did not prevent him from making use of " human nature " as a key to unlock all the doors which did not open to his analysis at the first pressure. But with Taine the appeal to human nature assumes another form. He does not talk about the phases of the evolution of the human individual, but instead he often, too often un-

[1] Madame de Staël often makes use of this analogy. " In investigating the three different epochs of Greek literature the natural progress of the human spirit is very clearly marked in them. In the most ancient period of their history the Greeks were famous for their poetry. Homer is characteristic of the first epoch of Greek literature. In the age of Pericles the rapid progress of dramatic art, rhetoric, morals and the beginnings of philosophy is observed. In the epoch of Alexander the deep study of the philosophic sciences becomes the chief occupation of the outstanding people in literature " (op. cit., I, p. 7-8). This is all true, but " the natural progress of the human spirit " is far from explaining for us the causes of such development.

fortunately, talks about race. " What is called race," he says, " is the innate and inherited qualities which a man brings with him into the world ".[1] There is nothing easier than to free oneself of all difficulties by attributing any complicated phenomenon to the activity of these innate and inherited qualities. But historical aesthetics suffers greatly from this.

Henry Sumner Maine was firmly convinced that in everything concerning social evolution there exist deep differences between the Aryan race and races of " another origin ". In spite of this he expressed a characteristic desire: " it is to be hoped that contemporary thought will before long make an effort to emancipate itself from those habits of lethargy in adopting theories of race which it seems to have contracted. Many of these theories appear to have little merit except the facility which they give for building on them inferences tremendously out of proportion to the mental labour which they cost the builder ".[2] It can only be hoped that this desire will be realised as soon as possible. Unhappily it is not so easy as it may appear at first glance. Maine says that " many, probably even the majority of the differences in the character of the nations forming the sub-divisions of the Aryan race are in reality only differences in the degree of its development ". This is undoubted. But

[1] Ibid., p. xxiii.
[2] Maine, " Lectures on the Early History of Institutions ", 6 éd., p. 96-97.

in order no longer to feel the need for the master key of the race theory it is necessary to understand correctly the features which characterise the different stages of development. But this is impossible, without a conception of history free of contradictions. Taine had no such conception. But are there many such historians and critics who do possess one?

Before us lies " Geschichte der deutschen national-literatur " of Dr. Hermann Klüger. This history, which is apparently pretty well known in Germany, has absolutely nothing remarkable about it in the shape of use value. But the periods into which the author divides the history of German literature invite our attention. We find the following seven periods in his book, (p. 7-8 of the 14th edition):

1. From the most ancient times to Charles the Great (800). This is chiefly the epoch of the ancient, pagan folk song and the period in which the old sagas of the heroes were formed.

2. From Charles the Great to the beginning of the 12th century (800-1100). In this period the ancient national paganism yields after a stern struggle to Christianity. Literature is chiefly under the influence of the clergy.

3. The first period of the flourishing of German literature from 1100-1300. Poetry chiefly develops and is cultivated by the knights.

4. The development of poetry in the hands of the

estate of small burghers and artisans, from 1300 to 1500.

5. German literature in the epoch of the Reformation (1500-1624).

6. Poetry in the hands of the men of learning; the epoch of imitation (1624-1748).

7. The second period of flourishing of German literature, beginning in 1748.

The German reader, more competent than ourselves, can himself judge upon the details of this division. But to us it appears absolutely eclectic, that is constructed not upon the basis of any principal which is the essential condition for any scientific classification and division, but on the basis of several, incommensurate principles. In the first periods literature develops apparently under the exclusive influence of religious ideas. Then come the third and fourth periods, in which its development is determined by social structure, by the condition of the classes which " cultivate " it. From 1500 religious ideas again become the chief lever in literary evolution : the century of the Reformation begins. But this hegemony of religious ideas is continued altogether only for a century and a half. In 1624 the men of learning seize the role of demiurge in German literature, etc. The division into periods which we have examined is at least as unfortunate as that used by Condorcet in his " Esquisse d'un tableau des progrès de l'esprit humain ". And the cause of this is the same. Klüger, like Condorcet, does not know on what depend social evolution and its consequence, the spiritual evolution of man. So we were right in stating that in this sphere our century has only made very modest progress.

But let us return to Taine again. " The general condition of things " under the influence of which this or that work of art arises is for him the general presence of definite benefits and definite ills, a condition of freedom or servitude, poverty or wealth, a definite form of society, a definite kind of religion. But the condition of freedom or slavery, of wealth or poverty and finally the form of society, these are the features which characterise the real condition of people " in the social production of their life ". Religion is the imaginative form in which their real condition is expressed in men's heads.

The latter is cause, the former effect. If one keeps to idealism the opposite may, of course, be maintained, that is, that people owe their real condition to religious ideas and then it is necessary to consider as cause what we take for effect. In any case, I hope it is necessary to recognise that it is impossible to put cause and effect together when we have to characterise " the general condition of things " in any given epoch, for this will lead to unbelievable confusion. Men's real condition is constantly lumped together with the general condition of their morals and their spirit or, to use other words, the understanding of the expression " general condition of things " is lost, and it is just against this obstacle that Taine collided and, in addition to him, a whole number of historians of art.[1]

[1] For example, here is the judgement of Charles Blanc on Dutch painting. " To sum up, we can say that three important causes, national independence, democracy and protestantism put their seal on the Dutch school. Emancipated from the Spanish yoke, the seven provinces began to develop their painting, freeing themselves in their turn from foreign style . . . the republican form of government once established freed it from purely decorative art as cultivated by courts and monarchs, from what is called decorative painting. Finally, family life which protestantism developed brought to life a number of splendid kinds of picture which have made Batavian painting famous forever, since it was necessary to decorate the walls of the intimate dwelling which had become altars for the lovers of art." (" Histoire des peintres de toutes époques," Paris 1861, I, p. 19-20.) Hegel said something very similar to this. " The Dutch in their religion were protestants, a very important fact, since protestantism alone was able to penetrate completely into the prose of life, and, independently of religious relations, fully value it and allow it to develop freely and without limitations ". (" Aesthetik ", II, p. 222.) It would not be difficult to show by quoting from Hegel himself that it would be much more logical to consider that it was not protestantism which exalted " the prose of life ", but, on the contrary, " the prose of bourgeois life ", having reached a definite stage of strength and development gave birth to protestantism in the course of its struggle against the " prose " or, if you like, the poetry of the feudal régime. If this is so then it is impossible to see a sufficient cause for the development of Dutch painting in protestantism. It is necessary to go further to some " third ", " higher " thing which gave birth both to the protestantism of the Dutch and their governments (" democracy "), about which Ch. Blanc speaks, as well as their art, etc.

The materialist conception of history finally frees us from all these contradictions. Although it gives us no magic formula (it would be ridiculous to demand one), which allows us to solve in a moment all the problems of the spiritual history of humanity, it nevertheless brings us out of the enchanted circle and points out to us the true task of scientific investigation.

We are convinced that not one of our readers will be sincerely surprised to hear from us that for Marx the problem of history was also in a certain sense a psychological problem. But nevertheless it is undoubted. As far back as 1845 Marx wrote: " The chief lack of materialistic philosophy up to the present, including that of Feuerbach, is that the thing, the reality, sensation is only conceived of under the form of the object which is presented to the eye, but not as human sense—activity, " praxis," not subjectively. It therefore came about that the active side in opposition to materialism was developed from idealism, but only abstractly; this was natural, since idealism does not recognise real tangible facts as such."[1]

What is the meaning of these words which to a certain extent contain the programme of modern materialism? They mean that if materialism does not wish to remain onesided, as it has done up to now, if it does not wish to betray its own principle and constantly return to idealist outlooks; if it does

[1] See the Appendix to Engels' " Ludwig Feuerbach ", " Marx on Feuerbach ".

not wish to recognise idealism as stronger in a definite sphere, it must know how to give a materialist explanation to all sides of human life. The subjective side of this life is precisely the psychological side, " the human spirit ", the sentiments and ideas of men. To examine this side from the materialist point of view means, in so far as it is a question of a definite aspect, to explain the history of ideas by the material conditions of men's existence, by economic history. Marx was all the more bound to point to the solution of the " psychological problem ", because he clearly saw into what an enchanted circle of confusion idealism had fallen in concerning itself with it.

So Marx says almost the same thing as Taine, only in rather different words. Let us see how Taine's " formula " must be changed in accordance with these other words.

The given stage of development of productive forces; the mutual relations of men in the social process of production, determined by this degree of development; the form of society, expressing these relations of men; the definite condition of spirit and morals corresponding to this form of society; religion, philosophy, literature, art, corresponding to the capacity, tendencies of taste and inclinations to which this condition has given birth—we would not say that this " formula " leaves nothing outside its limits,—far from it !—but it seems to us to have the undoubted advantage that it better expresses the causal connection existing between the different "links in the series". As for the "limitation" and "onesidedness", with which the materialist conception of history is usually reproached, the reader will find no trace of them in it.

Even the great German idealists, uncompromising enemies of any eclecticism, supposed that all aspects of the life of any nation are determined by one single principle. For Hegel this principle was a definite national spirit, "the general seal of the religion, political constitution, morality, system of law, customs, science, art, even technical capacities". Modern materialists considered this national spirit an abstraction, a product of thought that explained absolutely nothing. Marx rejected the idealistic conception of history. But this does not mean that he went back to the point of view of simple reciprocity which explains even less than the point of view of national spirit. His philosophy of history is also monistic, but in the sense diametrically opposed to the Hegelian. And it is just because of its monistic character that the eclectics see in it only limitation and onesidedness.

Perhaps the reader has noticed that by varying Taine's formula in accordance with the Marxist conception of history we have excluded what the French author calls "the dominant personality". We have done this deliberately. The structure of civilised societies is so complicated that it is impossible in the strict sense of the word to talk of a condition of spirit and customs corresponding to the given form of society. The condition of the spirit and customs of town-dwellers is often essentially different from the condition of agriculturists, while the spirit and customs of the nobility generally resemble very little the spirit and customs of the proletariat. Therefore a " personality " which is " dominant " in the imagination of one class is far from dominating in another. Could the courtier of the epoch of the " Roi soleil " serve as an ideal for the French peasant in the same epoch? Taine would undoubtedly object that it was not the peasant but aristocratic society which impressed its mark on the literature and art of France in the 17th century. And he would be absolutely right. The history of French literature in that century can consider the condition of the spirit and customs of the peasants a negligible quantity. But let us take another epoch, for example the epoch of the Restoration. Did one and the same " personality " " dominate " in the heads of the aristocracy of the period and in the heads of the bourgeoisie? Of course not. The bourgeoisie owing to its opposition to the supporters of the ancient régime not merely rejected the ideals of the aristocracy, but also idealised the spirit and manners of the Empire, the epoch of this same Napoleon which it had betrayed only a few years before.[1] As far back as 1789 the

[1] " The officials, artisans, shop-keepers undoubtedly considered it their duty to have a gloomy face and whiskers in order better to express their liberalism by their appearance. By their behaviour and certain trifles in their costume they thought

opposition to the bourgeois spirit and manners of the aristocracy made its appearance in the fine arts by the creation of the petty bourgeois drama. "What have I, a peaceful subject of a monarchical state in the 18th century, to do with revolutions in Athens and Rome? What real interest can I have in the death of a Peloponnesian tyrant or the sacrifice of a young princess of Aulis? There is nothing interesting in this for me, there is no moral which applies to me ", says Beaumarchais in his "Essais sur le genre dramatique sérieux ". And what he says is so true that one asks with astonishment how it was that the supporters of the pseudo-classical tragedy did not understand this. What did they see " in all this "? What moral did they find in it? Whereas the matter can be simply explained. In the pseudo-classical tragedy it was only apparently a question of a " Peloponnesian tyrant " or " a princess of Aulis ". In reality, to use an expression of Taine, it was only the subtly performed expression

to show that they were the fragments of our heroic army. The assistants in fashionable shops were not satisfied with moustaches; in order to complete their metamorphosis they stuck spurs on their boots which rang in military fashion on the stones of the roads and pavements of the boulevards " (A. Perlet, " De l'influence des mœurs sur la comédie ", 2 éd., Paris 1848, p. 52). We here have an example of the influence of the class struggle in a sphere which at first glance would seem to be dependent merely on caprice. It would be very interesting in a special work to examine the history of costume from the point of view of the psychology of classes.

of the aristocracy and evoked the delight of the latter. The new, coming world, the world of the bourgeoisie, respected this tragedy only out of tradition or else openly rebelled against it, for it was also rebelling against the " aristocracy " themselves. The leaders of the bourgeoisie thought that there was something humiliating to the dignity of a " citizen " in the rules of the old aesthetics. " To represent people from the lower estates in need and misfortune fie! fie! "— ironically exclaims Beaumarchais, in his " Lettres sur la Critique du Barbier de Seville ",—" they should be shown only in their capacity of abused persons. Citizens fit for laughter and unfortunate kings, this is the only possible dramatic spectacle, and I take note of it." The citizens who were Beaumarchais' contemporaries were at least in most cases the descendants of that French bourgeois who imitated the nobility with an assiduity worthy of better use and were laughed at for this by Molière, Dancour, Renoir and many others. So in the history of the spirit and manners of the French bourgeoisie we see at least two periods absolutely different from one another, the period of the imitation of the nobility and the period of opposi tion to it. Each of these periods corresponds to a definite phase in the development of the bourgeoisie. The inclinations and tendencies of taste in any class consequently depend upon the degree of its development and even more upon its relations to the higher class,—relations determined by the given development.

This means that the class struggle plays a great part in the history of ideas. And indeed, this part is so important that except for primitive societies in which classes do not exist, it is impossible to understand the history of the tendencies of tastes and ideas in any society without acquaintance with the class struggle taking place within it.

" The deepest characteristic feature of the whole process of development of modern philosophy," says Ueberweg, " is not simply the immanent dialectic of speculative principles, but rather the struggle and attempt at reconciliation, on the one hand, between outworn religious convictions which have nevertheless become deeply rooted in the spirit and feelings, and, on the other hand, the knowledge obtained thanks to modern researches, in the sphere of natural sciences and the sciences of the spirit."[1]

If Ueberweg had been more attentive he would have seen that at any given moment speculative principles have themselves been the result of the struggle and attempted conciliation of which he speaks. He should have gone further and asked himself the following questions :

1. Were not the traditional religious convictions the natural product of certain phases of social development;

2. Have not the discoveries in the sphere of natural sciences and sciences of the spirit, their source in the

[1] Ueberweg, " Grundriss der Geschichte der Philosophie ", hrsg. von Doctor Max Heinze. Berlin 1880, II Teil, p. 174.

preceding phases of this evolution; 3. Finally, has not this same evolution, which in one place and at one period of time has a quicker, and in another place and at another period, a slower rate and varies in dependence on a multitude of local conditions,—has it not caused both the struggle between religious doctrine and the new views acquired by modern thought, as well as the conciliation between the two forces leading the struggle, the speculative principles of which translate the conditions of this conciliation into the " holy language " of philosophy?

Examination of the history of philosophy from this point of view means an examination from a materialist point of view. Though Ueberweg was a materialist, in spite of his learning he had no idea of dialectical materialism. He has only left us what the historians of philosophy generally give us, the simple succession of the philosophical systems: such a system gave birth to such a one, while this latter in its turn gave birth to a third, and so on. But the succession of the philosophical systems is merely a fact, something granted, as they say to-day, which calls for explanation and which cannot be explained by " the immanent dialectic of speculative principles." For the men of the 18th century everything was explained by the activity of the legislators.[1] But we already know that

[1] " But why do the sciences know periods of stagnation during which the spirit ceases to be creative, and when it appears as though the nations have exhausted their extreme

this had as its cause social development. Shall we never succeed in bringing the history of ideas into connection with the history of societies, the world of ideas with the world of reality?

" Upon what a man is depends what philosophy he chooses for himself," says Fichte. Is it impossible to say the same about every society, or, more exactly, about every given social class? Surely we have the right to say with as firm a conviction, the philosophy of society or of a social class depends upon what that society or that class is?

Of course we should not forget here that if the ideas which prevail in any class at a given time are determined in their content by the social condition of that class, then in their form they are in close dependence upon the ideas which prevailed in the preceding epoch in the same or a higher class. " Tradition is a great conservative force in all spheres of ideology." (F. Engels.)

Let us look at socialism from this aspect. " Modern socialism is before all else the expression of the antagonism in the interests of the possessing classes and the proletarians, the workers and the bourgeois; and in the second place, the result of the anarchy prevailing in production. But in its theoretical form at first

productivity? Because disillusion is often the result of the imagined mistakes and weakness of the rulers." (" Tableaux des Révolutions de la Littérature Ancienne et Moderne." Par l'Abbé de Cournand, Paris 1786, p. 25.)

glance it appears really as the further development and apparently more consistent carrying out of the principles established by the great Encyclopaedists of the 18th century. Like every new theory socialism has to attach itself at first to the principles elaborated at the moment of its appearance. But the root, the real source of socialism lies in material economic facts."[1]

The formal but decisive influence of the complex of ideas which is already present makes itself felt not only in a positive sense, i.e., not only in the sense in which, for example, the French socialists in the first part of our century appealed to the same principles, and the Encyclopaedists in the preceding century, but this influence also assumes a negative character. If Fourier is constantly contending against what he ironically called the capacity for perfection capable of being perfected, he was doing so because this doctrine about the capacity of man for perfection played a great part in the theories of the Encyclopaedists. If the French Utopian socialists were on a good footing with the merciful God it proceeded from their opposition to the bourgeoisie which in this regard was distinguished in its youth by great scepticism. If these same Utopian socialists made political indifferentism into a principle, this arose from their opposition to the doctrine according to which " everything depends on legislation ". In a word, in the negative as well as in the positive sense, the formal side of the teaching of French social-

[1] Engels, " Anti-Dühring ", p. 1.

ism was determined by the theories of the Encyclopaedists and we should understand the latter properly
if we wish to understand the Utopians correctly.

What connection existed between the economic
situation of the French bourgeoisie in the epoch of the
restoration and the military appearance which the
petty-bourgeoisie, the knights of the yard measure of
that time, liked to give themselves? No direct connection. The moustaches and spurs in no wise
changed their condition either for the better or for the
worse. But we already know that this comical fashion
was indirectly created by the situation of the bourgeoisie
in comparison with that of the aristocracy. Many
phenomena in the ideological sphere can only be
indirectly explained through the influence of the
economic movement. This is very often forgotten not
only by the opponents but also by the supporters of
Marx's historical theory.

Since the evolution of ideology is essentially determined by economic development, both processes always
correspond to one another. " Public opinion " adapts
itself to economics, but this does not mean that in
studying the history of man we can take with equal
justice either side as our starting point, public opinion
or economics. Whilst economic development in its
general features can be satisfactorily explained by means
of its own logic, the path of spiritual evolution finds
its explanation only by means of economics. One
example will make our meaning clear.

In the time of Bacon and Descartes philosophy showed great interest in the development of productive forces. " Instead of that speculative philosophy which is taught in the Schools, we may find a practical philosophy by means of which, knowing the force and the action of fire, water, air, the stars, the heavens and all other bodies, that environ us, as distinctly as we know the different crafts of our artisans, we can in the same way employ them in all those uses to which they are adapted, and thus render ourselves the masters and possessors of nature."[1] The whole of Descartes' philosophy bears traces of this great interest. Thus, the aim of the investigations of modern philosophy was evidently clearly defined. But behold a century passes. Materialism,—which, it should be said here, is in general the logical consequence of Descartes' doctrine, —becomes wide-spread in France. The most progressive section of the bourgeoisie marches under its banner, a hot controversy is begun, but . . . they forget about productive forces. The materialist philosophers almost never spoke of them, they had quite other interests. It may appear as though philosophy had taken up quite different tasks. What is the cause of this change? Had productive forces in France not yet reached a sufficient development? Had the French materialists begun to despise the domination of man over nature of which Bacon and Descartes dream? Neither the one nor the other! But in Descartes' period productive

[1] Descartes, " Discours de la Methode ", Chap. VI.

relations in France, if we limit ourselves here to France alone, were still assisting the development of productive forces, whilst after the passage of a century they had become an obstacle to this.   It was necessary to destroy them and in order to destroy them it was necessary to attack the ideas which sanctified them.   The whole energy of the materialists, that advanced guard of the theoreticians of the bourgeoisie, was concentrated on this point, and their whole doctrine assumed a militant character.   The struggle against " superstition " in the name of " science " and against " tyranny " in the name of " natural law," was the most important, the most practical (in the Descartian sense) task of philosophy.   The direct study of nature having as its aim the rapid increase in productive forces passed into the background.   When the aim was achieved, when the worn-out productive relations were destroyed, philosophical thought assumed another direction, and for a long time materialism lost its importance.   The development of philosophy in France followed the changes in the country's economy.

" Unlike other builders, science not only plans castles in the air, but even puts on the different storeys before it lays the foundations ".[1]   Such behaviour appears illogical but it has its justification in the logic of social life.

When the 18th century " philosophers " remembered that man is the product of his environment they denied

[1] Marx, " Critique of Political Economy ".

254

any possibility of that same " public opinion " having influence on this environment, though in other cases, according to them, it rules the world. At every step their logic stumbled over one side or the other of this antinomy. Dialectical materialism solves it easily. For the dialectical materialists the opinion of men of course rules the world since in man, in the words of Engels, " all the impelling stimuli of his activity must be reflected in his head, being converted into the motives of his will ".[1] But this is not in contradiction to the fact that " public opinion " is rooted in the social environment and, in the last resort, in economic relationships. This is in no contradiction to the fact that any given " public opinion " begins to grow old in so far as the mode of production which called it forth also begins to grow old. Economics form " public opinion " which rules the world.

Helvétius, having made an effort to analyse " spirit " from the materialist point of view, failed owing to the complete inadequacy of his method. In order to remain true to his principle that " man is only sensation " Helvétius was forced to admit that the most famous giants of the spirit and the most glorious heroes of self-sacrifice for the public good acted, just like the most pitiful sycophants and ignoble egoists, merely for the sake of physical pleasures. Diderot protested against this paradox but could only depart from the conclusion drawn by Helvétius by finding a refuge in the sphere

[1] " Ludwig Feuerbach."

of idealism. However interesting was the effort of Helvétius, it nevertheless compromised in the eyes of the wide public and even of many " learned " persons, the materialist conception of " spirit ". There exists a deeply rooted idea that in this matter the materialist can only repeat what has already been said by Helvétius. It is, however, only necessary to understand " the spirit " of dialectical materialism to be convinced that the latter is answering for mistakes committed by its metaphysical predecessor.

Dialectical materialism examines phenomena in their development. But from the evolutionary point of view it is just as stupid to say that men consciously adapt their ideas and their moral feelings to their economic conditions as it is to declare that animals and plants consciously adapt their organs to the conditions of their existence. We are faced in both cases with an unconscious process to which a materialist explanation has to be given.

The man who has succeeded in finding a similar explanation of the origin of species has the following to say about " moral feeling " :

" It may be well first to premise that I do not wish to maintain that any strictly social animal, if its intellectual faculties were to become as active and as highly developed as in man, would require exactly the same moral sense as ours. In the same manner as various animals have some sense of duty though they admire widely different objects, so they might have a sense of right and wrong, though led by it to follow widely different lines of conduct. If, for instance, to take an extreme case, men were reared under precisely the same conditions as hive-bees there can hardly be a doubt that our unmarried females would, like the worker bees, think it a sacred duty to kill their brothers and mothers would strive to kill their fertile daughters; and no one would think of interfering. Nevertheless, the bee, or any other social animal, would gain in our supposed case, as it appears to me, some feeling of right or wrong, or a conscience. For each individual would have an inward sense of possessing certain stronger or more enduring instincts, and others less strong or enduring; so that there would often be a struggle as to which impulse should be followed; and satisfaction, dissatisfaction, or even misery would be felt, as past impressions were compared during their incessant passage through the mind. In this case an inward monitor would tell the animal that it would have been better to have followed the one impulse rather than the other. The one course ought to have been followed, and the other ought not; the one would have been right and the other wrong."[1] These lines almost started a prosecution against their author from " respectable " persons. A certain Sidgwick wrote in the London " Academy " that " a more highly developed bee " would strive to find a more gentle solution of the population question. We are ready to

[1] " The Descent of Man ", 1883, p. 99-100.

grant this with regard to the bee, but that the English bourgeoisie (and not only the English) did not find " a gentler " solution of the question is borne out by well-known books which are very respected by " respectable " persons. In June 1848 and in May 1871 the French bourgeoisie was far from being as gentle as " a more highly developed bee ". The bourgeoisie murdered (and commanded to be murdered) " their brothers " the workers with unheard-of cruelty and, what is even more interesting to us, with a perfectly calm conscience. They doubtless told themselves that they must follow precisely this " course " and not " another one ". Why? Because the morality of the bourgeois has been laid down for him by his social condition, his struggle against the proletarians, just as the " manner of action " of animals is dictated to them by the conditions of their existence.

These same French bourgeois consider the slavery of the ancients immoral and condemn the massacres of slaves who had risen in revolt in ancient Rome as being unworthy of civilised persons and even of bees gifted with reason. The bourgeois *comme il faut* is perfectly " moral " and devoted to the general good. But in his conception of morality and the general good he does not pass beyond the limits which have been shown to him, independently of his will and consciousness by the material conditions of his existence. And in this respect the bourgeois is in no way different from the members of other classes. Expressing in his ideas and feelings the material conditions of his existence, he merely undergoes the general fate of all " mortals ".

" Upon the different forms of property, upon the social conditions of existence, as foundation, there is built a superstructure of diversified and characteristic sentiments, illusions, habits of thought, and outlooks on life in general. The class as a whole creates and shapes them out of its material foundation, and out of the corresponding social relationships. The individual, in whom they arise through tradition and education, may fancy them to be the true determinates, the real origin, of his activities."[1]

Recently Jean Jaurès made an attempt at " a fundamental conciliation of economic materialism and idealism in their application to historical development ".[2] The brilliant orator was just a little late, since the Marxist conception of history leaves nothing to be " reconciled " in this sphere. Marx never shut his eyes to the part played by moral sentiments in history. But he explained the origin of these sentiments. So that Jaurès may better understand the sense of what he liked to call " Marx's formula ", though Marx always laughed at people with a formula, we will quote one more place from the above mentioned book.

[1] Marx, " The 18th Brumaire of Louis Bonaparte," p. 55.
[2] See his Lecture on the idealist conception of history. (" Neue Zeit ", XIII, 2, p. 545 ff.)

Marx is talking of the " social democratic " party which arose in France in 1849.

" The essential characteristic of social democracy is as follows. Democratic republican institutions are demanded as a means, not for the abolition of the two extremes, Capital and Wage Labour, but for the mitigation of their opposition, and for the transformation of their discord into a harmony. Various ways of attaining this harmony may be advocated, and the different proposals may be adorned with a more or less revolutionary trimming, but the substance is always the same. The substantial aim of social democracy is to transform society by the democratic method, the transformation being always kept within the petty bourgeois orbit. Do not run away with the idea that the deliberate purpose of the petty bourgeois class is to enforce its own selfish class interests. The petty bourgeois believe that the special conditions requisite for their own liberation are likewise the general conditions requisite for the salvation of modern society. They think that in no other way can society be saved and the class war averted. Nor must it be supposed that the democratic deputies are all shop-keepers, or enthusiastic champions of the small shop-keeper class. Culturally and by individual status they may be the polar opposites of members of the shop-keeping class. What has made them become the political representatives of the petty bourgeoisie is this. Intellectually they have failed to transcend the limitations which are, materially, imposed upon the petty bourgeois by the conditions of petty bourgeois existence. Consequently they are, in the theoretical field, impelled towards the same aspirations and solutions as those towards which in practical life, the petty bourgeois are impelled by material interests and by their social position. Speaking generally, such is always the relationship between the political and literary representatives of a class and the class they represent ".[1]

The superiority of the dialectical method of Marx's materialism is most clearly seen where it is a question of the solution of problems of a " moral " character, before which 18th century materialism came to a helpless stop. But in order to understand this solution correctly it is first of all necessary to get rid of metaphysical prejudices.

Jaurès again says: " I do not want to put the materialist conception on one side of the fence and the idealists on the other "; but he actually comes back to the system of " fences "; on the one side he puts spirit, on the other matter; on this side, economic necessity, on that side moral feeling, and then he preaches a sermon trying to prove that they must interpenetrate one another " as in the organic life of man the mechanism of the brain and conscious will interpenetrate one another ".[2]

[1] Ibid., p. 58.
[2] The reader who is curious to know how economic necessity penetrates " the idea of justice and right " will read

But Jaurès is not just any one. He possesses great knowledge, goodwill and remarkable abilities. You read him willingly (we have never had the pleasure of listening to him) even when he is mistaken. It is not possible, unfortunately, to say the same about the majority of Marx's opponents who fall over one another to attack him.

Herr Doctor Paul Bart, the author of the book " Die Geschichtsphilosophie Hegel's und der Hegelianer bis auf Marx und Hartmann," Leipzig 1890, has understood Marx so badly that he has managed to refute him. He has proved that the author of " Capital " contradicts himself at every step. Let us examine a little closer his method of proof. " In regard to the close of the Middle Ages Marx himself had given material

with great pleasure P. Lafargue's " Recherches sur les origines de l'idée du bien et du juste " in No. 9 of the " Revue philosophique ", 1858. We do not understand perfectly clearly what is meant by the penetration of economic necessity by the above mentioned idea. If by this Jaurès means that we must try to reorganise the economic relations of bourgeois society in accordance with our moral feelings, then we can answer him : 1. This goes without saying, but it would be hard to find in history a party which set itself the task of gaining the triumph of what, in its own opinion, would be in contradiction with " the idea of right and good ". 2. He does not take clearly into account the sense of the words he uses. He talks about morality which, to use Taine's expression, establishes dictates, whereas the Marxists, in what may be called their moral teaching, only try to state laws. In such conditions a misunderstanding is absolutely inevitable.

for his own refutation in declaring (' Kapital ', B. I, p. 737-750) that one of the chief causes of the primitive ' accumulation ' of capital was the driving of the English peasants off the land by the feudal lords who, owing to the rise in prices of wool, turned arable into sheep-pasture with just a few shepherds, the so-called enclosures, and the conversion of these peasants into proletarians standing outside the law so that they fell into the grip of developing manufacture.   Although, according to Marx, this agricultural revolution is explained by the rise of woollen manufacture, nevertheless, to use his own expression, the feudal forces, the landlords greedy for profit, were its violent levers (' Kapital ', B. I, p. 747), i.e. political force became a link in the chain of economic revolutions ".[1]

As we have more than once said, the 18th century philosophers were convinced that " everything depends on legislation ".   But when at the beginning of the 19th century it was recalled that the legislator to whom they had attributed all-powerfulness, is engendered in his turn by social environment; when they understood that " legislation " in any country is founded in its social structure, then a tendency to fall into the opposite extreme was frequently observed.   They often began to underestimate the role of the legislator which they had formerly overestimated.   For example, J. B. Say says in the preface to his " Traité d'économie politique ": " For a long time politics in the real sense of

[1] Op. cit., p. 49-50.

the word, i.e. the science of the organisation of society, was confused with political economy, with the teaching of how wealth arises, is distributed and consumed. But wealth in reality does not depend on political organisation. The state can flourish under any form of government if it is well ruled. Some nations have grown wealthy under absolute monarchs, others have perished under National Assemblies. If political freedom is favourable to the development of wealth, then it is only indirectly so, in the same way as it favours education ". The Utopian socialists went even further. They loudly declared that the reformer of social organisation should have nothing to do with politics.[1] Both these extremes have this in common, that both are rooted in the lack of a correct understanding of the connection existing between the social and political organisation of a country. Marx discovered the connection and so it was easy for him to show how and why every class struggle is also a political struggle.

[1] " In our civilised world we have all possible forms of government. But do the western countries, which are more or less inclined to a democratic form of state, suffer less from spiritual, moral and material poverty than the eastern countries which have a more or less autocratic form of government? Or has the Prussian monarch shown less kindness towards the lower classes of the nation than the French Chamber of Deputies or the King of the French? The facts prove so much the opposite, reflection convinces us so much of the opposite, that we regard all politically liberal efforts more than indifferently and they become merely objectionable to us." (M. Hess in the " Gesellschaftsspiegel ", 1846.)

The clever Doctor Bart has only seen one point in all this, that, according to Marx, political action, the " legislative " act cannot have any influence on economic relations; that, according to this same Marx, every such act is a simple appearance and that therefore any English peasant deprived by the landlord of his landed property " at the close of the Middle Ages ", i.e. deprived of his former economic condition, brings down in ruins like a house of cards the whole historical theory of the famous socialist. Voltaire's grocer from Salamanca was not cleverer than this!

So, Marx contradicts himself in his description of the " clearing of estates ". The superb logician, Herr Bart, makes use of this same clearing in order to show that law " has a self-sufficing existence ". Since the aim of the judicial action of the English landlords has very little in common with their economic interests, the honourable Doctor makes a statement which is certainly free from any onesidedness. " So law has a self-sufficing, proper, although not independent existence." Self-sufficing, although not independent! This is certainly many sided and what is even more important, protects our Doctor from any " contradictions ". If people begin to prove to him that law is conditioned by economics, he will answer, that is because it is not independent. If, on the other hand, it is explained to him that economics is determined by law, then he will answer that this is just what his theory of the self-sufficient existence of law desires to prove.

The clever doctor affirms the same thing concerning morality, religion, and all other ideology. Everything, without exception, is self-sufficient although not independent. You see this is the old but ever fresh story of the struggle of eclecticism against monism, the story of the " fences ": here is matter, there is spirit,—two substances which have a self-sufficient, proper, though not independent existence.

But let us leave the eclecticians and return to the theory of Marx. We have a few further remarks to make on it.

Savage tribes, whether peaceful or not peaceful, have relations among themselves, and, if opportunity offers, with barbarian nations and civilised states. These relations, naturally, exercise an influence on the economic structure of any society. " Different communities discover in their natural environment different means of production and different means of subsistence. Consequently their methods of production, modes of life, and products, are different. It is owing to the existence of these spontaneously developed differences that when communities come into contact, there occurs an exchange in their several products one for another, so that these products gradually become transformed into commodities ".[1] The development of commodity production leads to the destruction of the

[1] " Capital ", Vol. I, p. 371.

primitive commune. In the depths of the clan there arise new interests which finally give birth to a new political organisation. Class struggle begins with all its inevitable consequences in the sphere of the political, moral and intellectual evolution of humanity. Its international relations become ever more complicated and give birth to phenomena which at first glance contradict Marx's historical theory.

Peter the Great carried out a revolution in Russia which had a tremendous influence on the economic development of that country. But not economic needs, but needs of a political character, the needs of the state inspired this man of genius to his revolutionary acts. In the same way the defeat in the Crimea forced the government of Alexander II to do all in its power to develop Russian capitalism. History teems with similar examples which apparently bear witness in favour of the self-sufficient existence of international, state and any other kind of law. But let us examine things a little more closely. On what depended the strength of the West European states which inspired the genius of the great Muscovite? On the development of their productive forces. Peter understood this very well, since he did everything to assist the development of these forces in his own country. Whence did he get the means which he had at his disposition; whence rose the power of the Asiatic despot which he wielded with such terrible energy? This power owed its origin to the economics of Russia.

These means were limited by the production relations existing in Russia at that time. In spite of his terrible power and his iron will Peter did not succeed and could not succeed in turning St. Petersburg into Amsterdam or converting Russia into a sea power, as was his constant dream. The reforms of Peter the Great gave birth in Russia to a peculiar phenomenon. Peter tried to start European manufactures in Russia, but there were no workers in the country. He forced state serfs to work in the manufactories. Industrial serfdom, a form unknown in Western Europe, existed in Russia up to 1861, i.e. until the emancipation of the serfs from serfdom.

A no less characteristic example is the feudal condition of the peasants in East Prussia, Brandenburg, Pomerania and Silesia, existing since the middle of the 16th century. The development of capitalism in western countries undermined in a planned way the feudal forms of the exploitation of the producers. In the above-mentioned corner of Europe its development confirmed them for a fairly long period of time.

Slavery in the European colonies in the same way at first glance appeared to be a paradoxical example of capitalist development. This phenomenon, like those mentioned above, cannot be explained by the logic of the economic life of those countries in which it appeared. To explain it, it is necessary to examine international economic relations.

So we here, in our turn, have gone back to the point of view of reciprocity. It would be stupid to forget that this is not merely a legitimate but also an absolutely essential point of view. It would only be a similar stupidity to forget that this point of view in itself explains nothing and that in making use of it we must always seek the " third ", " higher " thing, that which for Hegel was idea, and for us, the economic condition of the nations and countries, the mutual influence of which it is necessary to state and understand.

Literature and the fine arts in any civilised country have a greater or lesser influence on the literature and the fine arts of other civilised countries. This reciprocal influence is the result of the similarity of the social structures of these countries.

A class which is in a state of struggle with its adversaries wins a position for itself in the literature of its country. If this same class begins to come into movement in another country it assimilates the ideas and forms created by its more advanced brothers. But it varies them or goes further than they do, or lags behind them in dependence on the difference existing between its position and the position of the class whose example it has followed.

We have already seen that geographical environment has a great influence on the historical development of nations. Now we see that international relations have a still greater influence on this development. The united influence of geographical environment and international relations explains to us the immense difference to be seen in the historical fates of nations in spite of the fact that the main laws of social evolution are everywhere the same. It appears that the Marxist conception of history, being neither "limited" nor "onesided", opens out an immense field of investigation for us. Much labour, patience and love of truth is necessary in order to cultivate properly even a very small part of this field. But it belongs to us. The achievement has been made, the work has been begun by the hands of incomparable masters and we have only to continue it. And we must do so unless we wish to transform inside our heads Marx's idea of genius into something "grey", "gloomy", "dead".

"But if thought never gets further than the universality of the Idea, as perforce was the case in the first philosophies (when Eclectics never got beyond Being, or Heraclitus beyond Becoming), it is justly open to the charge of formalism. Even in a more advanced phase of philosophy, we may often find a doctrine which has mastered merely certain abstract propositions or formuli, such as, 'in the absolute all is one', 'subject and object are identical', and only repeating the same thing when it comes to particulars".[1] With complete justice we might be

---

[1] "Encyklopädie", I Teil, Paragraph 12, Einleitung.

accused of similar formalism if we had merely repeated in regard to any given society that the anatomy of this society is founded in its economics. This is indisputable. But this is insufficient. It is necessary to know how to make a scientific use of a scientific idea, it is necessary to be able to take into account all the vital functions of an organism the anatomical structure of which is determined by economics. It is necessary to understand how it moves, how it is nourished, how the sensations and conceptions arising in it thanks to its anatomical structure become what they are. It is necessary to understand how they change together with the changes which take place in its structure, etc. It is only on this condition that we can go forward. But by merely observing this condition we can have full confidence.

People often see in the materialist conception of history a doctrine which proclaims man's subjection to the yoke of an uncompromising, blind necessity. It would be difficult to find a more perverse idea. It is precisely the materialist conception of history which shows men the course leading from the kingdom of necessity into the kingdom of freedom.

In the sphere of morality, the philistine, an eclectic par excellence, is always an "idealist". He clings to his "ideal" with the greater obstinacy the more help-less his reason feels itself in the presence of the wretched prose of social life. Thus, reason will never triumph over economic necessity, the ideal will always remain the ideal; it will never be realised since it " has a self-sufficient, proper, although not independent existence ", since it is impossible for it to pass beyond the limits of its " fences ". On this side, the spirit, the ideal, human dignity, fraternity etc.; on that side, matter, economic necessity, exploitation, competition, crises, bankruptcy, mutual universal deception. It is impossible to reconcile these two kingdoms. Modern materialists can only behave with contempt towards such " moral idealism ". They have a much higher conception of the power of human reason. True, the latter moves forward in its development only thanks to economic necessity, but precisely for that reason the really reasonable must not remain for ever in the condition of the " ideal ".

What is reasonable becomes real, and the whole insurmountable force of economic necessity assumes the realisation of this.

The 18th century " philosophers " repeated *ad nauseam* that public opinion rules the world and that therefore nothing can oppose reason which " in the last resort is always right." And nevertheless these philosophers often showed great doubts in the power of reason and their doubts arose logically out of the other side of the theory characteristic of the " philosophers ". Since everything depends on the " legislator " he either allows reason to triumph or else extinguishes its torch. It is therefore necessary to place all hopes in the " legislator ". But in the majority of cases the legislators, the monarchs, who have the fate of their nations in their hands, are very little interested in the triumph of reason. Thus the appearances of reason become very poor ones! It only remains for the philosopher to count upon chance which will sooner or later place power in the hands of a " sovereign " friendly to reason. We have already seen that Helvétius in fact counted only upon a happy chance. Let us hear one more philosopher of the same period.

" The most undoubted principles most often encounter objections. They contend with ignorance, lack of faith, commonness, human obstinacy and vanity, in a word—with the interests of the powerful of the world and with popular stupidity which compel them to maintain the old systems. Error defends its territory step by step. Only by struggle and effort can the most insignificant conquests be wrenched from it. We cannot from this draw the conclusion that truth is useless. The seed sown by it is preserved; in time it brings forth fruit and, like the seeds which wait a long time in the earth for their sprouting, it awaits the circumstances which will allow it to develop. . . . When an enlightened sovereign begins to rule the nations truth brings forth the fruits which have been quite rightly expected of it. Finally necessity compels the nations, worn out with poverty and endless unhappy chances, caused by their mistakes, to find a refuge in truth which can alone protect them from the misfortune from which they have long suffered owing to lies and prejudice."[1]

Here is the same belief in the " enlightened despot ". Here is the same doubt in the power of " reason ". Just compare these fruitless and timid hopes with the unwavering conviction of Marx who tells us that there is not and never will be a sovereign who could offer successful opposition to the development of the productive forces of his people and, consequently, to its emancipation from the oppression of worn-out institutions, and then say : who believes more strongly in the power of reason and its final triumph?   On the one hand, a careful " perhaps ", on the other—confidence just as unshakable as that which we get from mathematical proof.

The materialists could only half believe in their god " reason " since, according to their theory, the god was continually stumbling against the iron laws of the material world, against blind necessity.   " Man achieves his end," Holbach says, " without being free for a moment, commencing at his birth and finishing with his death."[2]   The materialist has to make such a declaration since, in the words of Priestley, " the doctrine of necessity is the immediate result of the

[1] " Essais sur les préjugés, de l'influence des opinions sur les mœurs et sur le bonheur des hommes etc." Liège 1797, p. 37.   This book is attributed to Holbach or to the materialist Dumarsais whose name is on the title page.

[2] " Le bon sens puisé dans la nature ", I, p. 12.

doctrine of the materiality of man; for mechanism is the undoubted consequence of materialism."[1]

Until they had understood how this necessity might create human freedom they had inevitably to be fatalists. "All phenomena are connected with one another," says Helvétius. "The cutting down of a forest in the north changes the direction of the winds, the condition of the sown earth, the arts of a country, its manners and government." Holbach speaks of the endless consequences which the movement of a single atom in the brain of a despot may have for the faith of a State. The determinism of the " philosophers " did not go any farther in misunderstanding of the role of necessity in history. For them therefore, historical necessity was subject to chance, that small change of necessity. Freedom remained in contradiction with necessity and materialism was unable, as Marx showed, to understand human activity. The German idealists saw clearly this weak side of metaphysical materialism, but they succeeded, with the help of the absolute spirit, i.e. of a fiction, in uniting freedom with necessity. Modern materialists like Moleschott revolve in the contradictions of the 18th century materialists. Only Marx was able, without for a moment renouncing the doctrine of the " materiality of man ", to reconcile " reason " and " necessity " by examining " human practise ". "Mankind always takes up only such

[1] Priestley, " A free discussion of the principles of material-ism ", p. 241.

problems as it can solve; since, looking at the matter more closely, we will always find that the problem itself arises only when the material conditions necessary for its solution already exist or are at least in the process of formation."[1]

The materialist metaphysicians saw how necessity subjects people to itself (" the cutting down of a forest " etc.); dialectical materialism shows how they may be emancipated.

" The bourgeois relations of production are the last antagonistic form of the social process of production— antagonistic not in the sense of individual antagonism, but of one arising from conditions surrounding the life of individuals in society; at the same time the productive forces developing in the womb of bourgeois society, create the material conditions for the solution of that antagonism. This social formation constitutes, therefore, the closing chapter of the prehistoric stage of society."[2]

The so-called fatalistic theory of Marx in fact has for the first time in the history of economic science put an end to that fetishism of the economists which explained economic categories—exchange value, money, capital—by the nature of material objects and not by the relations of men in the process of production.[3]

---

[1] " Critique of Political Economy ", p. 12-13.

[2] Ibid., p. 13.

[3] " The extent to which certain economists have been led astray by the fetishistic character that attaches to the world of

We cannot here explain all that Marx did for political economy. We will simply remark that in this science he made use of the same method and in its treatment stood on the same point of view as in his explanation of history, the point of view of the relations of men in the process of production. It is possible, therefore, to judge the intellectual level of the people, commodity, the manner in which they have been deluded by the semblance of objective material reality that is assumed by the social attributes of labour, is shown (to give one instance among many) by the wearisome and absurd dispute concerning the part played by nature in the creation of exchange value; since exchange value is nothing more than a specific social way of expressing the labour that has been applied to a thing, it cannot contain any more natural (material) substance than does, for instance, the rate of exchange.

" The commodity form is the most general and least developed form of bourgeois production. For this reason, it makes its appearance early though in a less dominant and typical manner than to-day. For this reason, likewise, the fetishistic character of commodities is comparatively easy to discern. But when we come to more developed forms, even this semblance of simplicity vanishes. Whence did the illusion of the monetary system arise? The mercantilists (champions of the monetary system) regarded gold and silver, not simply as substances, which, when functioning as money, represented a social relation of production, but as substances which were endowed by nature with peculiar social property. Later economists, who look back upon the mercantilists with contempt, are manifestly subject to the very same fetishistic illusion as soon as they come to contemplate capital. It is not so very long since the dispelling of the physiocratic illusion that land rents are a growth of the soil, instead of being a product of social activity ! " (" Capital ", Vol. I, p. 57.)

particularly numerous in modern Russia, who " recognise " Marx's economic theories and " refute " his historical views.

He who has understood what is the dialectical method of Marx's materialism can also judge the scientific value of the disputes which arise from time to time upon what kind of method Marx made use of in his " Capital "—the inductive or the deductive.

Marx's method is at once both inductive and deductive, but it is in addition the most revolutionary of all methods which have ever been applied.

" In its mystified form, dialectic became the fashion in Germany because it seemed to elucidate the existing state of affairs.   In its rational form it is a scandal and an abomination to the bourgeoisie and its doctrinaire spokesmen, because, while supplying a positive understanding of the existing state of things, it at the same time furnishes an understanding of the negation of that state of things, and enables us to recognise that that state of things will inevitably break up; it is an abomination to them because it regards every historically developed social form as in fluid movement, as transient; because it lets nothing overawe it, but is in its very nature critical and revolutionary."[1]

Holbach, one of the most revolutionary representatives of 18th century French philosophy, was frightened by the struggle for markets without which the modern bourgeoisie is unable to exist. He would willingly have

[1] " Capital ", Vol. I, p. 874.

held up historical development in this respect. Marx welcomes this struggle for markets, this greed for profit, as a force which is breaking down the existing order of things, as the premise of the emancipation of humanity.

" The bourgeoisie cannot exist without constantly revolutionising the instruments of production, and thereby the relations of production, and with them the whole relations of society. Conservation of the old modes of production in unaltered form, was, on the contrary, the first condition of existence for all earlier industrial classes. Constant revolutionising of production, uninterrupted disturbance of all social conditions, everlasting uncertainty and agitation distinguish the bourgeois epoch from all earlier ones. All fixed, fast frozen relations, with their train of ancient and venerable prejudices and opinions, are swept away, all new formed ones become antiquated before they can ossify. All that is solid melts into air, all that is holy is profaned, and man is at last compelled to face with sober senses his real conditions of life and his relations with his kind.

" The need of a constantly expanding market for its products chases the bourgeoisie over the whole surface of the globe. It must nestle everywhere, settle everywhere, establish connections everywhere.

" The bourgeoisie has through its exploitation of the world market given a cosmopolitan character to production and consumption in every country. . . . In place of the old local and national seclusion and self-sufficiency, we have intercourse in every direction, universal inter-dependence of nations. And as in material, so also in intellectual production. The intellectual creations of individual nations become common property. National onesidedness and narrow-mindedness become more and more impossible, and from the numerous national and local literature there arises a world literature."[1]

In their struggle against feudal property, the French materialists sang the praises of bourgeois property, which in their opinion was the innermost soul of every human society. They only saw one side of the matter. They considered bourgeois property to be the fruit of the labour of the property owner himself. Marx shows where the immanent dialectic of bourgeois property ends.

" The average price of wage labour is the minimum wage, i.e. that quantum of the means of subsistence which is absolutely requisite to keep the labourer in bare existence as a labourer. What, therefore, the wage labourer appropriates by means of his labour, merely suffices to prolong and reproduce a bare existence. We by no means intend to abolish this personal appropriation of the products of labour, an appropriation that is made for the maintenance of reproduction of human life, and that leaves no surplus wherewith to command the labour of others. . . . In existing society,

[1] " Communist Manifesto ", p. 12-13.

private property is already done away with for nine-tenths of the population; its existence for the few is solely due to its non-existence in the hands of those nine-tenths."[1]

However revolutionary the French materialists may have been, they appealed only to the enlightened bourgeoisie and to the " philosophising " nobles who were passing over into the camp of the bourgeoisie. They showed an insurmountable fear of the " mass ", the people, the " ignorant mob ", but the bourgeoisie was and could be only half revolutionary. Marx appeals to the proletariat, to the revolutionary class in the full sense of that word.

" All the preceding classes that got the upper hand, sought to fortify their already acquired status by subjecting society at large to their conditions of appropriation. The proletarians cannot become masters of the productive forces of society, except by abolishing their own previous mode of appropriation, and thereby also every other previous mode of appropriation. They have nothing of their own to secure and to fortify; their mission is to destroy all previous securities for, and insurance about individual property."[2]

[1] Ibid., p. 24-25. The law of wages about which Marx here speaks is more exactly formulated in " Capital ". He there shows that it is in reality still more unfavourable for the proletarian. But what is said in the " Manifesto " is sufficient to destroy the illusion which the 19th century inherited from its predecessor, or more correctly, from its predecessors.

[2] " Communist Manifesto ", p. 20.

In their struggle against the social order then existing the materialists appealed to the " powerful of this world ", to the " enlightened despots ". They tried to show them that their theories were really quite harmless. Marx and the Marxists have quite another attitude towards " the powerful of this world."

" The Communists disdain to conceal their views and aims. They openly declare that their ends can be attained only by the forcible overthrow of all existing social conditions. Let the ruling classes tremble at a communist revolution. The proletarians have nothing to lose but their chains. They have a world to win."[1]

It is perfectly understandable that such a doctrine could not meet with a favourable reception from the " powerful of this world ". The bourgeoisie has become in our day a reactionary class. It is trying " to turn back the wheel of history ". Its ideology is no longer in a condition to understand the immense scientific importance of Marx's discoveries. Therefore the proletariat utilises his historical theory as a trusty guide in its struggle for emancipation.

This theory, while frightening the bourgeoisie by the so-called fatalism attaching to it, fills the proletariat with unexampled energy. Defending the " doctrine of necessity " from Price's attacks, Priestley says : " To say nothing of myself, who certainly, however, am not the most torpid or lifeless of all animals; where will he find greater ardour of mind, a stronger and more

[1] " Communist Manifesto ", p. 44.

unremitted exertion, or a more strenuous and steady pursuit of the most important objects, than among those of whom he knows to be necessarians? "[1]

Priestley is speaking of the English Christian necessarians who were his contemporaries. He might or might not be justified in attributing such enthusiasm to them. But even a little conversation with Messieurs Bismarck, Caprivi, Crispi, or Casimir Perier will tell you of the miracles of activity and energy of the " necessarians " and " fatalists " of our time—the social-democratic workers.

[1] Op. cit., p. 391.

INDEX